# BEEF WITH TOMATO

## DEAN HASPIEL

HANG DAI EDITIONS • ALTERNATIVE COMICS

# CONTENTS

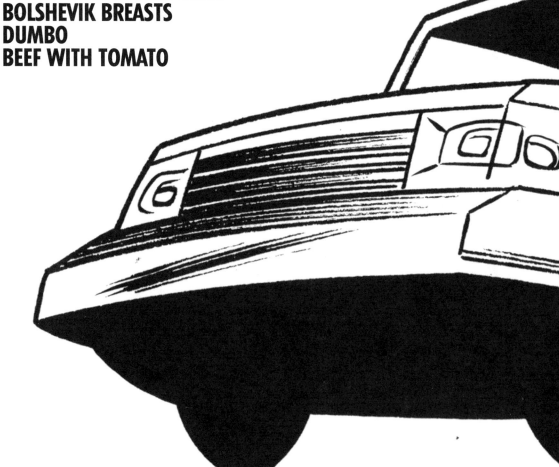

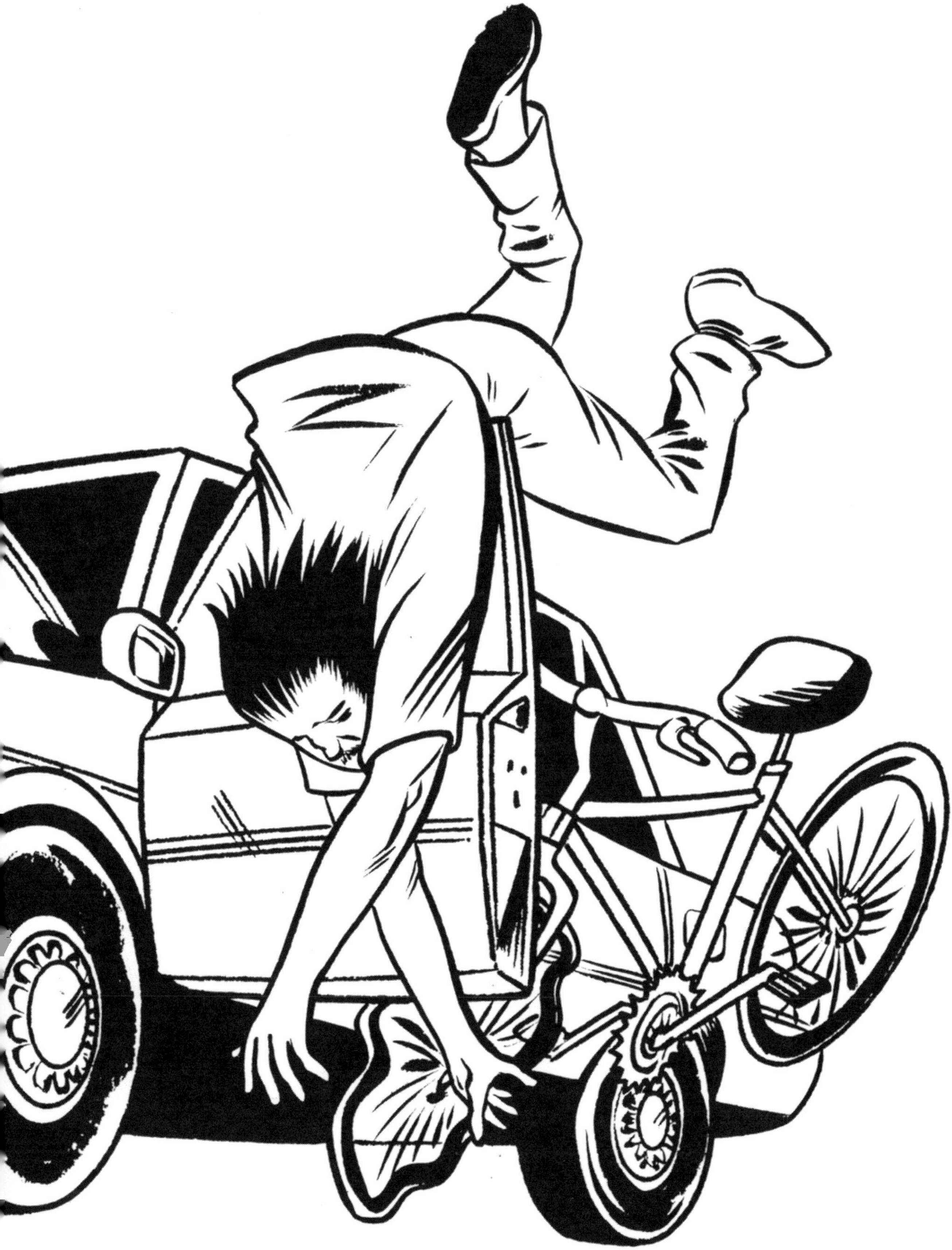

Thanks to: Harvey Pekar, Josh Neufeld,
Jonathan Ames, Jen Ferguson, Gregory
Benton, Seth Kushner, Nick Bertozzi,
Larry O'Neil, Mike Hueston, Tim Hall,
Linda Perkins, Julia Durkot, Sarah
Butterworth, Jonah Kaplan, Seth
Dinnerman, Vanessa Wieman, Christa
Cassano, Barbara Haspiel, James Haspiel,
Kwanza Johnson, Ron Perazza, Jack Mahan,
Jeff Mason, Stephen Elliott, Jonathan
Santlofer, Zack Zook, Eric Skillman,
Marc Arsenault, J51 Posse, Trip City,
Yaddo, and Hang Dai Studios.

Published by:
Alternative Comics
21607B Stevens Creek Blvd.
Cupertino, California 95014
IndyWorld.com

Hang Dai Editions
Brooklyn, NY
hangdaieditions.com

Printed in the United States of America

ISBN:
978-1-934460-81-8

deanhaspiel.com

# INTRODUCTION

## JONATHAN AMES

I met Dean Haspiel in 2001. He came up to me in a café on Smith Street in Brooklyn. He said he had read and enjoyed a column I used to write for the (now defunct) New York Press. He went on to tell me that I should read his comics and that we should be friends. Dean is a very gregarious and confident person. I did what he said. I read his comics and became his friend. I'm very glad I listened to him on both fronts.

I love the book you are holding. It's Dean on the streets of New York. His adventures, his scuffles, his heartbreaks. As he wheels about on his bicycle—his crumpled nose at the prow of his one-man ship, his chest hair held in check by a black t-shirt and black jacket—he records and takes in the city like a camera that makes comics.

He's a witness, a diarist, and a documentarian. There's comedy and beauty in every panel of this book. Please delight in the shadows, the faces, the angles, the stories—he infuses each moment with a wonder and curiosity that is both hard-boiled and tender. He likes to think of himself as a bruiser, but really – well, this is my opinion—he's a poet. A poet who wants to fight the good fight, which means more often than not that you drop your fists, you cry, you go home, and you draw.

*Renaissance man, Jonathan Ames is the author of such novels and essay collections as* Wake Up, Sir!, The Extra Man, What's Not To Love?, *and creator of HBO's* Bored To Death, *and Starz's* Blunt Talk. *Jonathan also collaborated with Dean Haspiel on their graphic novel,* The Alcoholic.

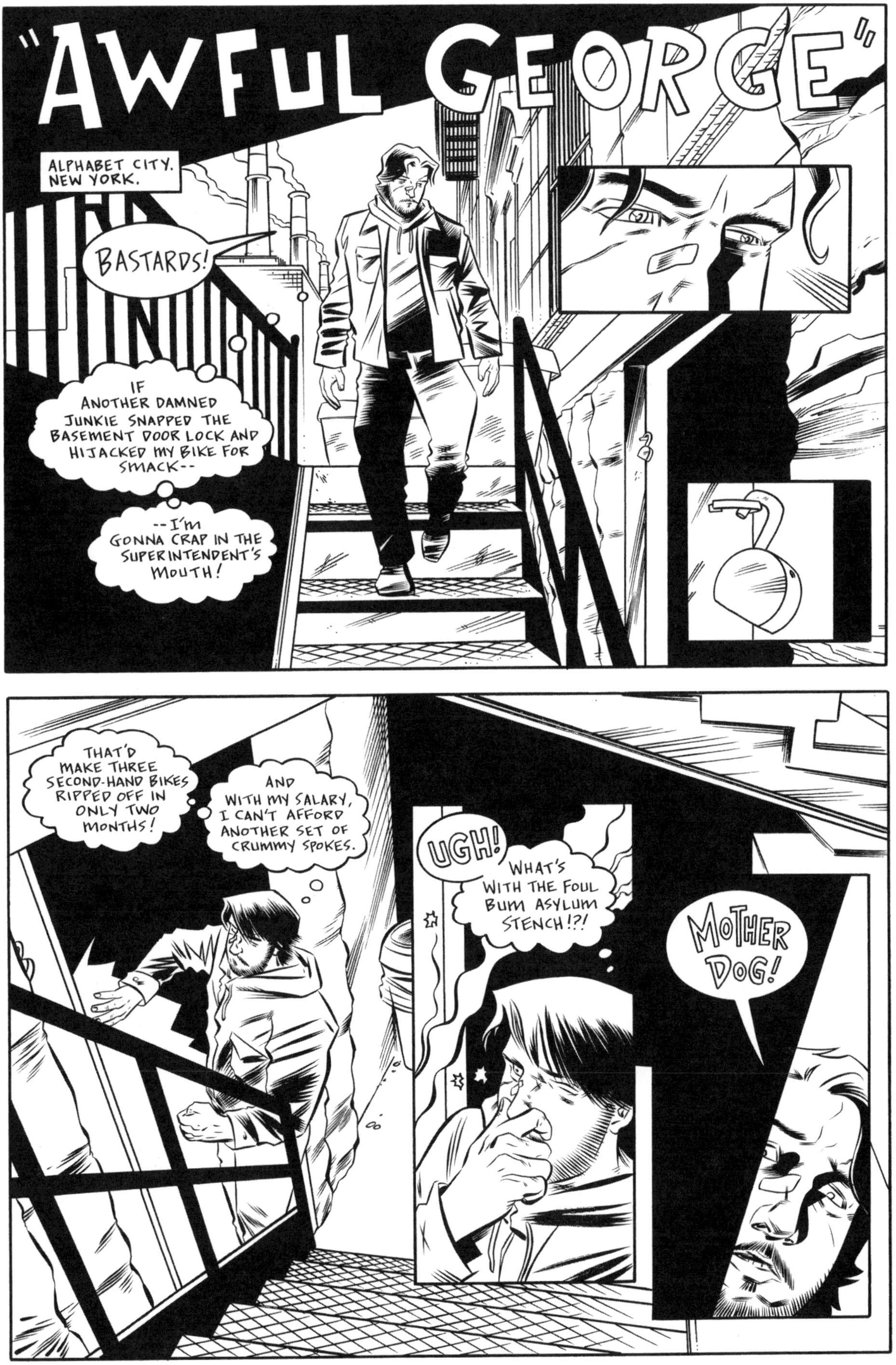
"AWFUL GEORGE"
ALPHABET CITY. NEW YORK.
BASTARDS!
IF ANOTHER DAMNED JUNKIE SNAPPED THE BASEMENT DOOR LOCK AND HIJACKED MY BIKE FOR SMACK--
--I'M GONNA CRAP IN THE SUPERINTENDENT'S MOUTH!
THAT'D MAKE THREE SECOND-HAND BIKES RIPPED OFF IN ONLY TWO MONTHS!
AND WITH MY SALARY, I CAN'T AFFORD ANOTHER SET OF CRUMMY SPOKES.
UGH!
WHAT'S WITH THE FOUL BUM ASYLUM STENCH!?!
MOTHER DOG!

I WAS CONFRONTED BY THE STARTLING SIGHT OF A WOMAN FRANTICALLY PERFORMING IMPROMPTU SURGERY ON A KITTY CAT WHILE STANDING OVER A MAKESHIFT OPERATING TABLE MADE FROM MILK CRATES AND A BROKEN REFRIGERATOR DOOR.

BLOODY TOWELS AND BOWLS OF WATER WITH ARCHAIC METAL INSTRUMENTS OF VARYING DEGREES OF HORROR WERE STREWN ABOUT THE SPACE.

CROWDING THE SPACE WERE METAL CAGES HOUSING TWO-TO-THREE CATS IN EACH ONE. THE CATS WERE EITHER HALFWAY TO HEAVEN OR HALFWAY TO HELL.

SOME CATS WERE MISSING AN EYEBALL OR A TAIL. OTHERS WERE MISSING A LIMB AND/OR TEETH. ALL OF THEM WERE IN PAIN AND SUFFERING.

BIKES AND BOXES OF VALUABLES WERE SAFELY STASHED IN THE BACK OF THE BASEMENT. NOTHING WAS STOLEN FROM THE PREMISES, ONLY ADDED TO.

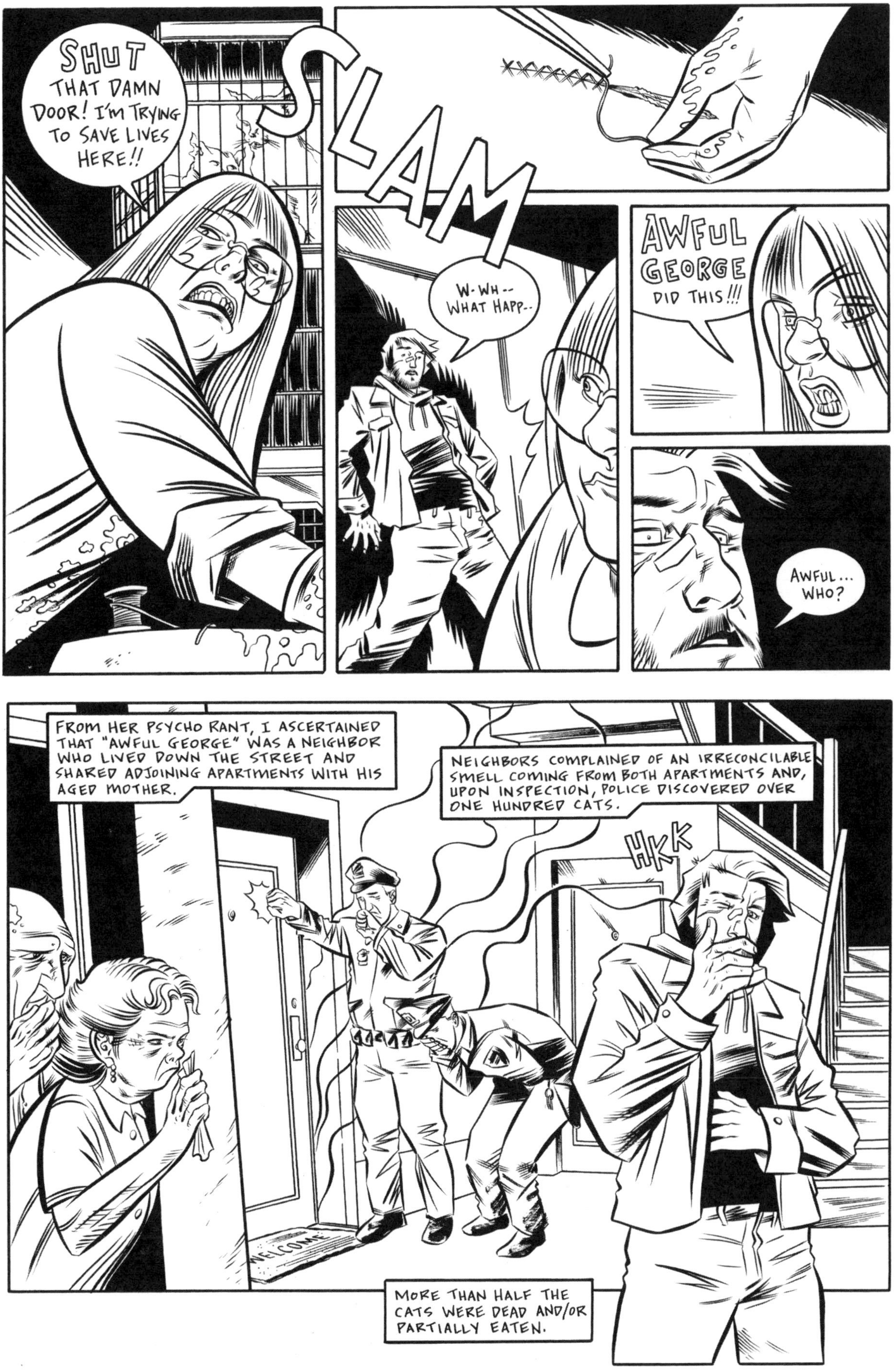
SHUT THAT DAMN DOOR! I'M TRYING TO SAVE LIVES HERE!!
SLAM
W-WH-- WHAT HAPP--
AWFUL GEORGE DID THIS!!!
AWFUL... WHO?
FROM HER PSYCHO RANT, I ASCERTAINED THAT "AWFUL GEORGE" WAS A NEIGHBOR WHO LIVED DOWN THE STREET AND SHARED ADJOINING APARTMENTS WITH HIS AGED MOTHER.
NEIGHBORS COMPLAINED OF AN IRRECONCILABLE SMELL COMING FROM BOTH APARTMENTS AND, UPON INSPECTION, POLICE DISCOVERED OVER ONE HUNDRED CATS.
HKK
WELCOME
MORE THAN HALF THE CATS WERE DEAD AND/OR PARTIALLY EATEN.

THE SURVIVING CATS HAD SPLINTERED OFF INTO SAVAGE TRIBES, KILLING EACH OTHER FOR FOOD, TERRITORY, ETC.

THE ONES THAT WERE DISEASE RIDDEN WERE DESTROYED.

THE RADICAL ANIMAL RIGHTS ACTIVIST WHO STOOD BEHIND ME ADOPTED THE REMAINING CATS...

...AND SHE WAS TRYING TO SAVE MORE THAN JUST NINE LIVES.

FOR A WEEK, I VISITED THE FELINE TRIAGE TO BLESS THE CATS WITH HEARTFELT ENCOURAGEMENT TO LIVE!

IT'S GOING TO BE OKAY. YOU'RE GOING TO MAKE IT.

HK KK

I PAID EXTRA ATTENTION TO MY OWN CATS IN THE SAFETY AND COMFORT OF MY APARTMENT.

IT'S GOING TO BE OKAY. YOU'RE GOING TO MAKE IT.

I SOUGHT COUNCIL FROM MY GIRLFRIEND.

BUT, WHAT IF..?

SHHH. IT'S GOING TO BE OKAY. YOU'RE GOING TO MAKE IT.

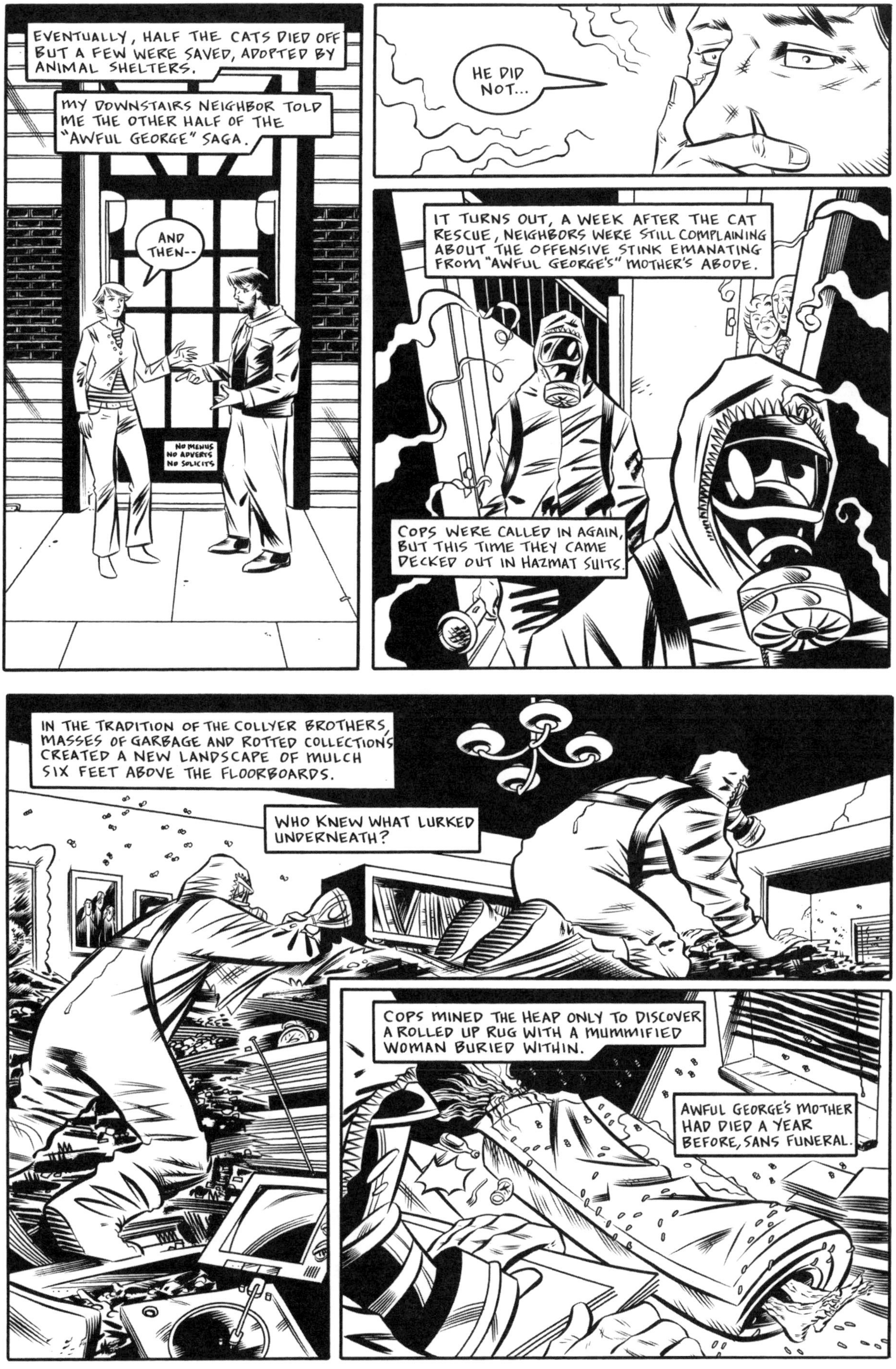
EVENTUALLY, HALF THE CATS DIED OFF BUT A FEW WERE SAVED, ADOPTED BY ANIMAL SHELTERS.
MY DOWNSTAIRS NEIGHBOR TOLD ME THE OTHER HALF OF THE "AWFUL GEORGE" SAGA.
AND THEN--
NO MENUS
NO ADVERTS
NO SOLICITS
HE DID NOT...
IT TURNS OUT, A WEEK AFTER THE CAT RESCUE, NEIGHBORS WERE STILL COMPLAINING ABOUT THE OFFENSIVE STINK EMANATING FROM "AWFUL GEORGE'S" MOTHER'S ABODE.
COPS WERE CALLED IN AGAIN, BUT THIS TIME THEY CAME DECKED OUT IN HAZMAT SUITS.
IN THE TRADITION OF THE COLLYER BROTHERS, MASSES OF GARBAGE AND ROTTED COLLECTIONS CREATED A NEW LANDSCAPE OF MULCH SIX FEET ABOVE THE FLOORBOARDS.
WHO KNEW WHAT LURKED UNDERNEATH?
COPS MINED THE HEAP ONLY TO DISCOVER A ROLLED UP RUG WITH A MUMMIFIED WOMAN BURIED WITHIN.
AWFUL GEORGE'S MOTHER HAD DIED A YEAR BEFORE, SANS FUNERAL.

NOSY NEIGHBORS DISCOVERED THAT THERE HAD BEEN NO RECORD OF HER BURIAL.

ERGO, THE ETERNAL RANK OF DEATH BETRAYING COVERT ASYLUM.

THE BROKE AND LONELY BASTARD WAS PULLING AN "ED GEIN" IN NEW YORK CITY!

DID YOU HEAR THAT?

HEAR WHAT?

BZZT

SOMETHING ...MOVED.

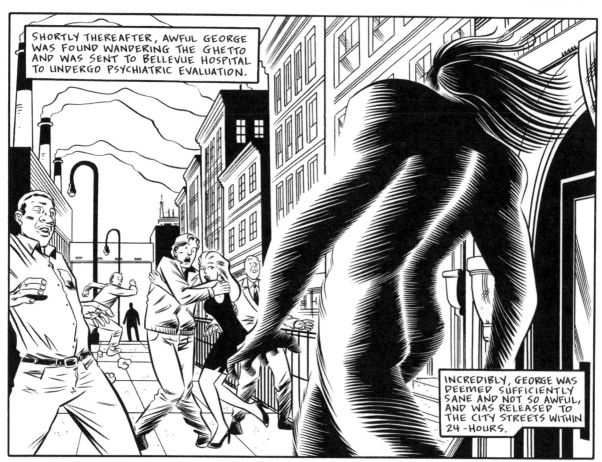

SHORTLY THEREAFTER, AWFUL GEORGE WAS FOUND WANDERING THE GHETTO AND WAS SENT TO BELLEVUE HOSPITAL TO UNDERGO PSYCHIATRIC EVALUATION.

INCREDIBLY, GEORGE WAS DEEMED SUFFICIENTLY SANE AND NOT SO AWFUL, AND WAS RELEASED TO THE CITY STREETS WITHIN 24-HOURS.

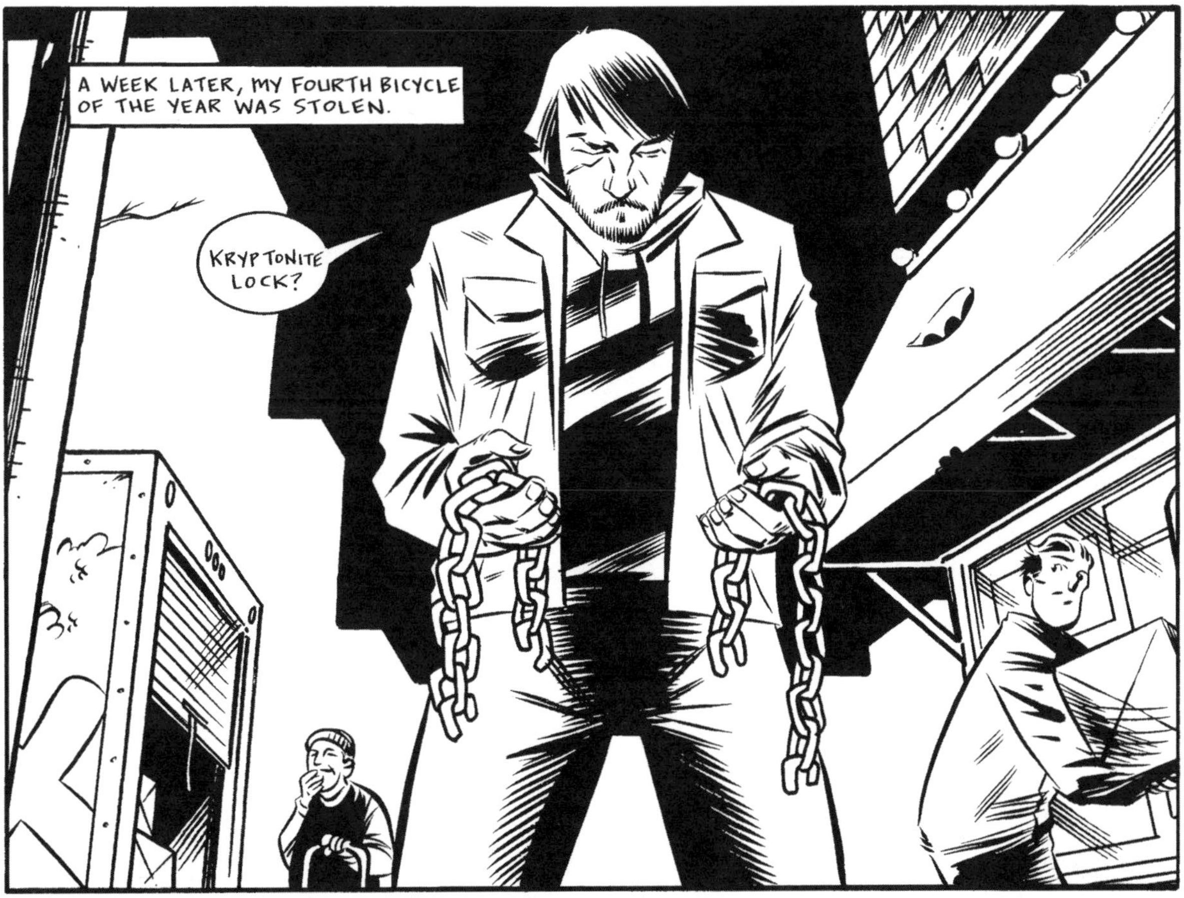
A WEEK LATER, MY FOURTH BICYCLE OF THE YEAR WAS STOLEN.
KRYPTONITE LOCK?

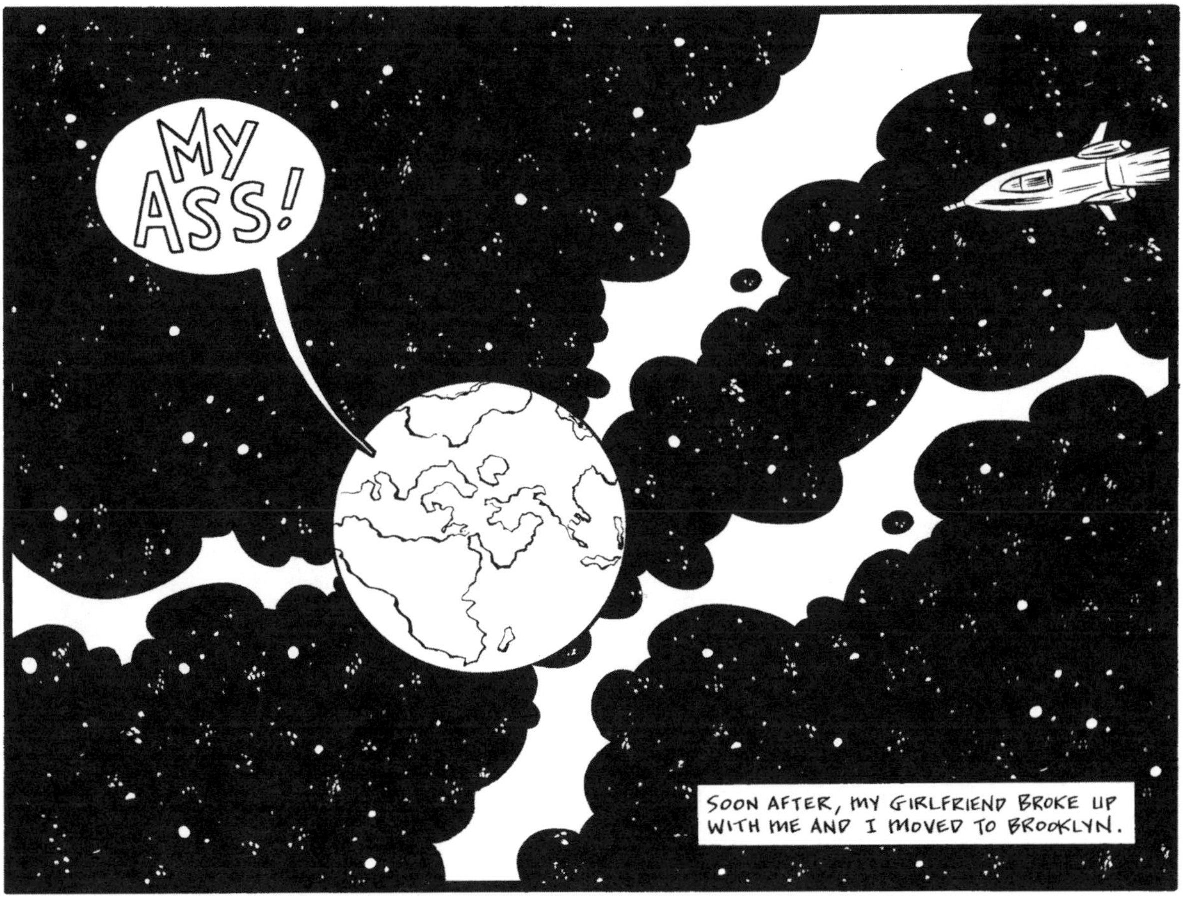
MY ASS!
SOON AFTER, MY GIRLFRIEND BROKE UP WITH ME AND I MOVED TO BROOKLYN.

I LEARNED THAT MY NEW DIGS ON CARROLL STREET IN BROOKLYN WAS PRIMARILY ITALIAN.

IN FACT, CARROLL GARDENS USED TO BE A PART OF RED HOOK BEFORE REAL ESTATE DECIDED TO RID THIS SECTION OF ITS HISTORICAL RELATION TO AL CAPONE, GANGSTERS, AND SHIP WORKERS BY LETTING THE BQE (BROOKLYN QUEENS EXPRESSWAY) DIVIDE THE NEIGHBORHOOD.

"OLD SCHOOL"

RED HOOK.

CARROLL GARDENS.

WHEN I FIRST WALKED DOWN MY BLOCK TO SURVEY THE NEIGHBORHOOD, I WOULD GET THE HAIRY EYEBALL FROM OLD ITALIAN MEN WITH WALKING CANES WHOSE FACES LOOKED LIKE WRINKLED BASEBALL MITTS IN WOOL CAPS.

SOMETIMES I'D HEAR A GRUNT OR A POORLY DISGUISED COUGH THAT DECLARED ME "YUPPIE" AS IF I WERE SOME RICH TRUST FUND KID FROM THE UPPER EAST SIDE.

YUPPIE

IF ONLY THEY COULD SEE MY BANK ACCOUNT. NEVER MIND THE FACT THAT I DON'T HAVE HEALTH INSURANCE.

14

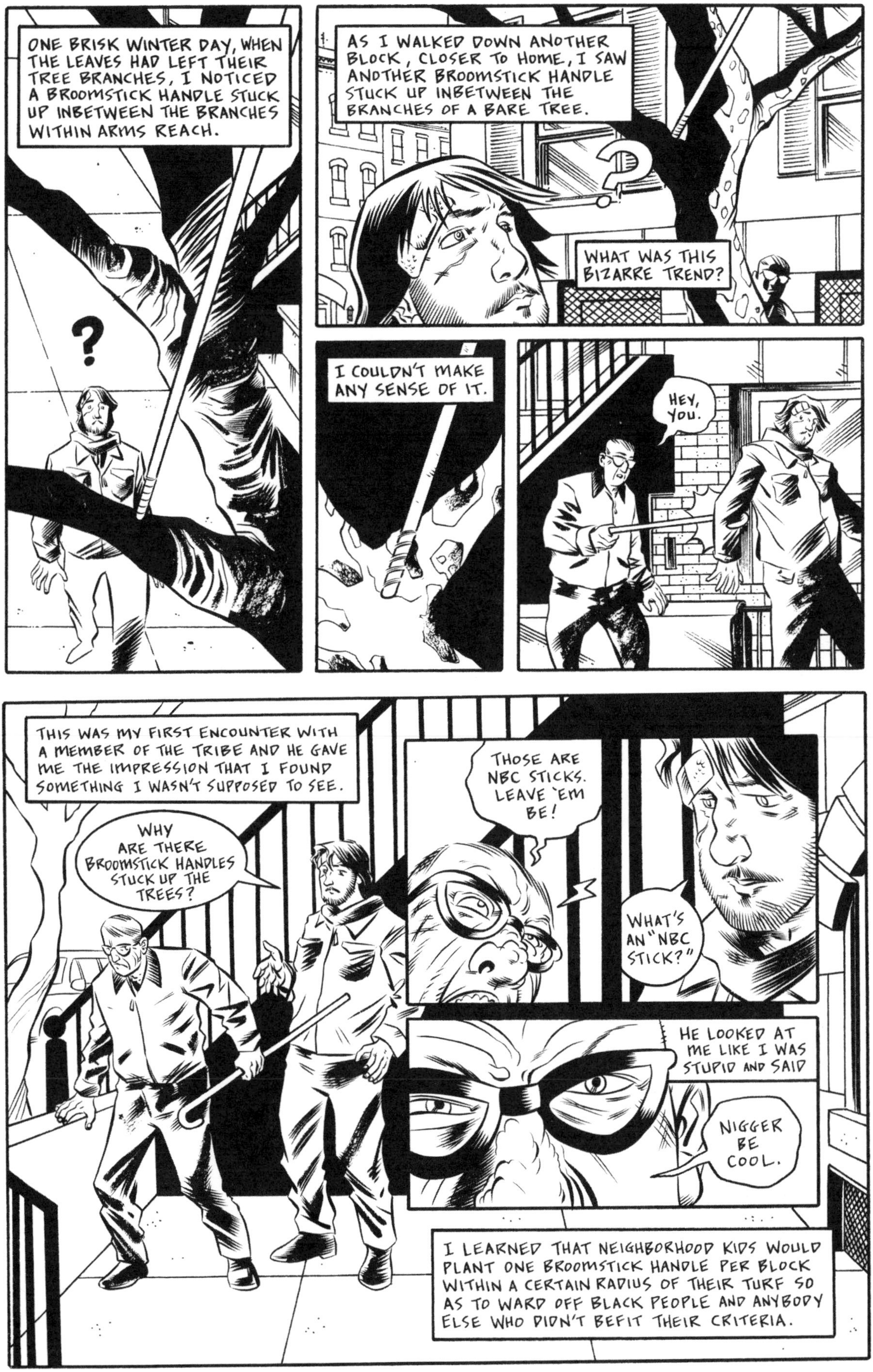

ONE BRISK WINTER DAY, WHEN THE LEAVES HAD LEFT THEIR TREE BRANCHES, I NOTICED A BROOMSTICK HANDLE STUCK UP INBETWEEN THE BRANCHES WITHIN ARMS REACH.
?
AS I WALKED DOWN ANOTHER BLOCK, CLOSER TO HOME, I SAW ANOTHER BROOMSTICK HANDLE STUCK UP INBETWEEN THE BRANCHES OF A BARE TREE.
?
WHAT WAS THIS BIZARRE TREND?
I COULDN'T MAKE ANY SENSE OF IT.
HEY, YOU.
THIS WAS MY FIRST ENCOUNTER WITH A MEMBER OF THE TRIBE AND HE GAVE ME THE IMPRESSION THAT I FOUND SOMETHING I WASN'T SUPPOSED TO SEE.
WHY ARE THERE BROOMSTICK HANDLES STUCK UP THE TREES?
THOSE ARE NBC STICKS. LEAVE `EM BE!
WHAT'S AN "NBC STICK?"
HE LOOKED AT ME LIKE I WAS STUPID AND SAID
NIGGER BE COOL.
I LEARNED THAT NEIGHBORHOOD KIDS WOULD PLANT ONE BROOMSTICK HANDLE PER BLOCK WITHIN A CERTAIN RADIUS OF THEIR TURF SO AS TO WARD OFF BLACK PEOPLE AND ANYBODY ELSE WHO DIDN'T BEFIT THEIR CRITERIA.

SOON AFTER, I GOT FRIENDLY WITH A MIDDLE-AGED POLISH PLUMBER WHO SAT DESHEVELED AND SWATHED IN GREASE ON HIS STOOP EVERYDAY STINKING UP THE BROWNSTONE WITH HIS DELI COFFEE AND CIGARETTES--

--WHILE HIS DOUBLE-PARKED VAN AWAITED RADIO CALLS FOR THE NEXT CLOGGED TOILET OR BURST PIPE.

OUR CASUAL NODS GRADUATED TO AN ACTUAL--

H'LO.

AND, FINALLY, CONVERSATION ABOUT WEATHER.

WHEN THE WEATHER WAS TOO NICE TO COMPLAIN ABOUT HE WOULD COMPLAIN ABOUT TAXES AND THE GOVERNMENT.

WHEN JULY 4TH ROLLED AROUND, HE GOT REAL PISSED OFF WHEN MOST EVERYBODY TAPED PAPER-MADE AMERICAN FLAGS TO THEIR APARTMENT WINDOWS AND CAR WINDSHIELDS.

WHY ARE YOU SO ANGRY ABOUT THAT?

PAPER FLAGS ARE CRAP!

IF THERE'S TWO THINGS PEOPLE SHOULD OWN IN THEIR HOME IT'S THE BIBLE AND A REAL AMERICAN FLAG MADE FROM CLOTH!

A WEEK LATER, KOREAN FEMALE TWINS MOVED NEXT DOOR TO ME. NOT ONLY DID THEY LOOK EXACTLY THE SAME, THEY HAD THE SAME HAIRCUT, THE SAME FASHION SENSE, AND THEY HAD THE SAME NAME, TOO!

EVERY SO OFTEN I'D GET A KNOCK ON MY DOOR BECAUSE ONE OF THE TWINS LIKED MY CATS AND WANTED TO PET THEM.

I COULD NEVER TELL IF THEY WERE SWITCHING BACK AND FORTH BETWEEN EACH OTHER TO MESS WITH ME --

-- BUT WE GOT FRIENDLY, ANYWAY.

ONE LUCID NIGHT I GOT EXPANSIVE AND COMPLAINED ABOUT MY BREAK UP WITH MY GIRLFRIEND BACK IN MANHATTAN AND THE KOREAN CAT LOVER LOOKED AT ME AGHAST!

WHAT'S THE MATTER?

YOU LIVE ALONE WITH TWO CATS.

YEAH, SO?

I'M SORRY. I THOUGHT YOU WERE GAY?

THE END.

SEPTEMBER 12, 2001. CARROLL GARDENS. BROOKLYN, NEW YORK.

I COULDN'T GIVE BLOOD BECAUSE HOSPITAL LINES WERE FIVE HOURS LONG AND LOCALS WERE ADVISED AGAINST CHARGING INTO MANHATTAN TO HELP EXCAVATE SURVIVORS FROM "GROUND ZERO."

HARD-WIRED TO HELP, TOO MANY PEOPLE WERE PULLING TOGETHER TO MOBILIZE -- AND THAT LEFT ME FEELING UTTERLY USELESS.

I WAS REDUCED TO A FEEBLE CAGE OF HUMAN STATIC AND EMOTIONAL INERTIA.

THESE WERE THE EMASCULATING FEELINGS I BASKED IN THE DAY AFTER THE HARROWING ATTACKS.

FEELINGS THAT WOULD ULTIMATELY GREASE MY AWARENESS AND INFORM MY BEHAVIOR AS A COMMON MAN SHARING COMMON SPACE --

-- WITH NOT SO COMMON PEOPLE.

HAVING SPENT A DAY AND A HALF, MOSTLY ALONE, TORTURED BY UGLY YET SOBERING THOUGHTS ABOUT TERRITORY AND CONTROL AND THE HORRIBLE TRUTH ABOUT HOW THE REAL WORLD REALLY FUNCTIONS --

-- I NEEDED RELIEF FROM A HEAVY HEART.

I NEEDED A VACATION FROM REPEATEDLY STARING AT MY TIRED TRAIN WRECK OF A FACE.

WHAT I WANTED WAS A FRIENDLY PARLAY WITH PALS TO ALLOW ME A RANT OR TWO AND A PLACE TO POUR OUT A LITTLE LIQUOR FOR "THE BROTHERS WHO CAN'T BE WITH US."

WHICH IS WHERE I WAS HEADING ON MY TRUSTY BIKE, WHEN, WHAT I GOT WAS --

DOORED

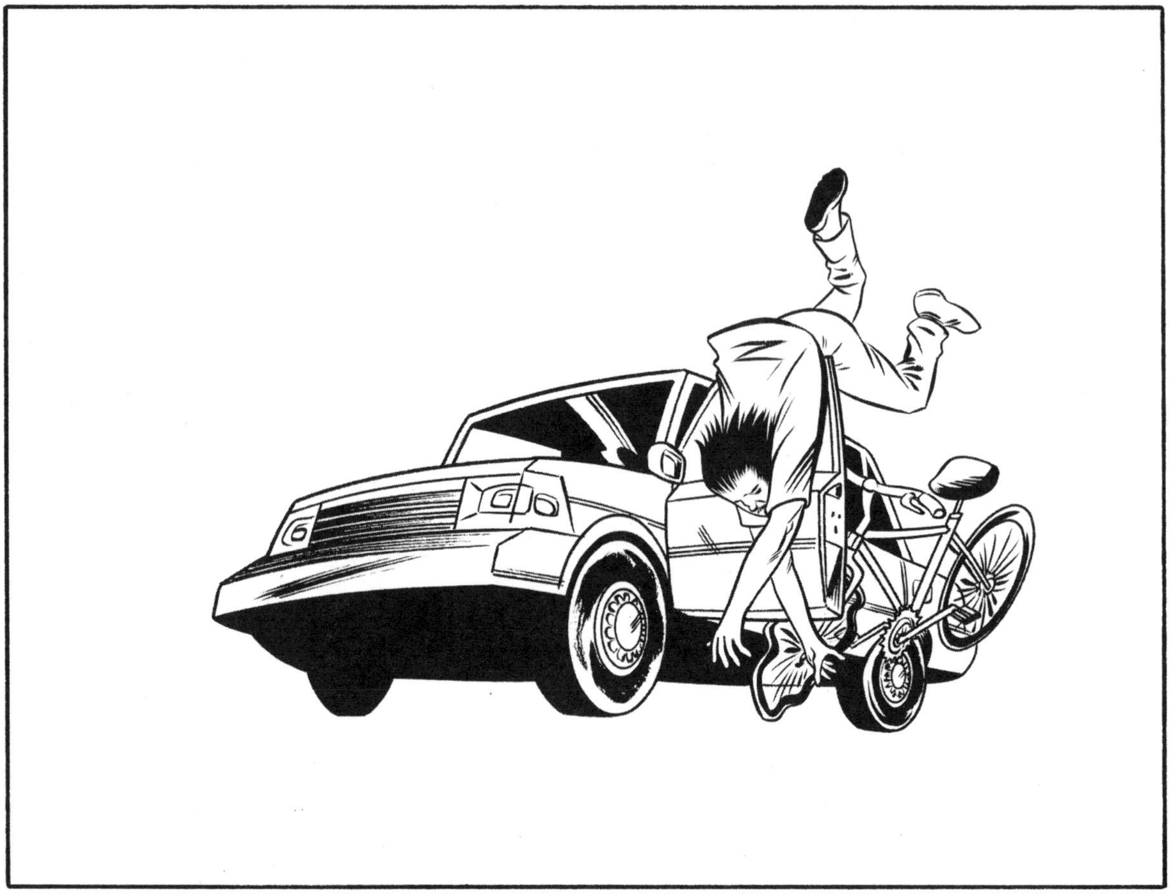

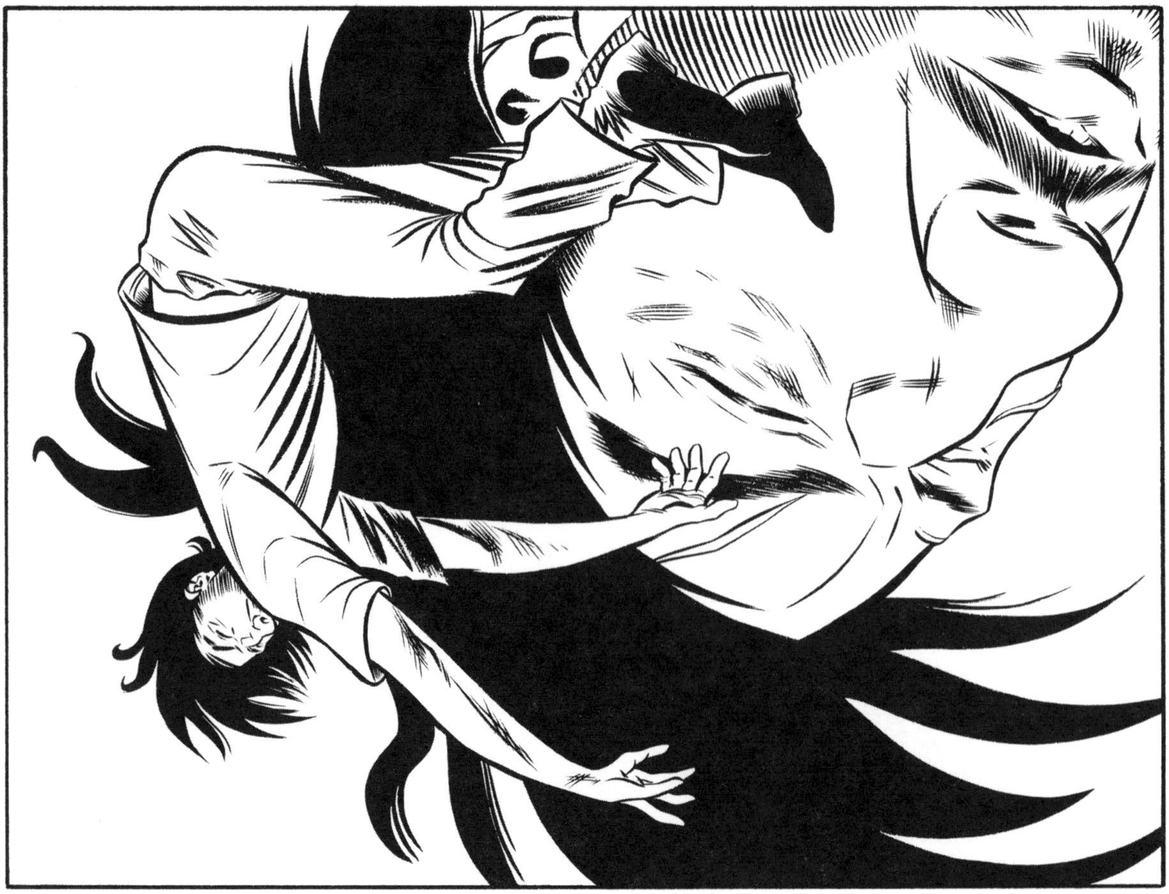

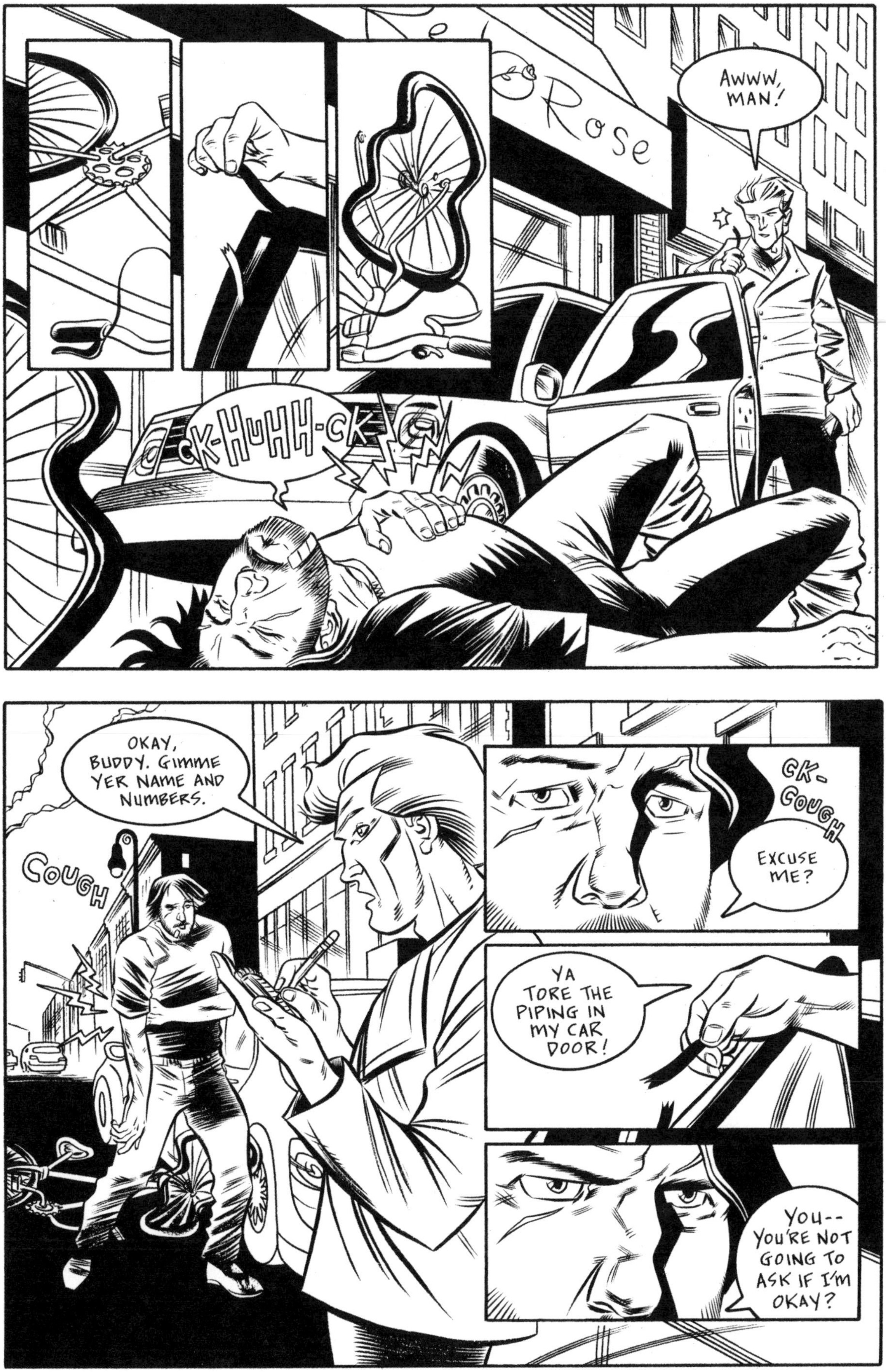
Rose
AWWW, MAN!
CK-HUHH-CK
OKAY, BUDDY. GIMME YER NAME AND NUMBERS.
COUGH
CK-COUGH
EXCUSE ME?
YA TORE THE PIPING IN MY CAR DOOR!
YOU-- YOU'RE NOT GOING TO ASK IF I'M OKAY?

IT'S OBVIOUS YER "OKAY." YER STANDIN' UP, AREN'T YA?

YOU DON'T CARE, DO YOU?

AFTER ALL THAT HAPPENED YESTERDAY.

MY HAND IS BLEEDING. MY CHEST HURTS AND MY BIKE IS BENT IN HALF.

AND YOU DON'T CARE?

LISTEN, MY DOOR MIGHT BE MORE THAN JUST SCRATCHED--

-- AND I NEED YER NAME AND NUMBERS.

UNLESS YA WANNA GO AND TAKE IT TO COURT?

♪ RIGHT ♫ FELLAH'S?

ARE YOU THREATENING TO TAKE ME TO COURT OVER A SCRATCH ON A CAR DOOR YOU MADE HAPPEN?

YOU KNOW WHAT--

--LET'S GO TO COURT--

--RIGHT NOW!

WOOP WOOP

DON'T MAKE ME SAY 1-2-3!

TURNS OUT A FEW WITNESSES SAW THE ACCIDENT AND VOUCHED FOR ME, STATING THAT THE BELLIGERENT LINE COOK WAS OUT OF LINE.

TO MAKE MATTERS SILLY, THE LINE COOK TRIED TO BEND HIS DOOR BEYOND ITS LIMIT TO CLAIM MORE DAMAGES FOR INSURANCE.

KRAK

THE COPS WERE IN AWE OF HIS AUDACITY.

23

THE COPS ADVISED ME TO FILL OUT AN ACCIDENT REPORT AND GO TO THE LOCAL EMERGENCY ROOM FOR X-RAYS AND BANDAGES.

THANKS.

AS SOON AS THE INITIAL SHOCK WORE OFF AND THE ADRENALINE SUBSIDED, I REALLY STARTED TO HURT.

I TOOK THE COPS' ADVICE AND CALLED THE HOSPITAL, EXPLAINING MY INJURIES, ASKING IF I SHOULD COME IN.

MY "DILEMMA" WAS MET WITH LETHARGY.

SURE... COME ON IN...

CLK

AND THEN IT HIT ME. HARD. I FELT A SUDDEN WAVE OF SHAME.

HOW DARE I TAKE UP THE SPACE OR THE TIME THAT SURVIVORS FROM A MAJOR DISASTER WOULD NEED!

INSTEAD, I WOULD BUCK UP AND BITE THE BULLET.

TAKE AN ASPIRIN AND BE ECSTATIC THAT I WAS ALIVE.

THE END.

24

I'M RIDING MY BIKE IN CARROLL GARDENS WHEN MY HIP VIBRATES WITH A DIGITAL JINGLE.

I SKID TO A STOP NEAR A SCHOOLYARD TO ANSWER MY CELL PHONE AND, BY THE TIME I FLIP OPEN MY CLAM SHELL, THE SIGNAL GOES DEAD.

"MASTER PLAN"

THAT'S WHEN THE RUBBER BOUNCE OF A BALL CATCHES MY EAR AND MY EYES SNAP TO THE LEFT.

MACK

I SEE A BASKETBALL SMACKING CONCRETE AND MAKING SMALL HOPS...

...AS IT DRIBBLES TOWARDS ME...

...LIKE A MAGNET.

I LOOK UP AND SEE A HULK OF A BLACK MAN WALKING TOWARDS ME.

I SHOULD FEEL A SENSE OF DANGER BUT THERE IS A PUZZLE PIECE MISSING TO THIS PICTURE.

I FEEL LIKE A HOOK CAUGHT IN A GILL.

GREAT.

THE HULK BENDS DOWN AND THAT'S WHEN THE REVEAL IS MADE.

BEHIND HIM, A GOOD 30-FEET AWAY, IS A WHEELCHAIR PARKED UNDER A BASKETBALL HOOP.

IN THE WHEELCHAIR IS A LITTLE BOY WEARING THICK EYEGLASSES.

HIS ARMS ARE MANGLED YET SPAZ AND WRIGGLE UNCONTROLLABLY WITH HYPER ACTIVITY.

HE HAS STUMPS WHERE HIS LEGS SHOULD BE.

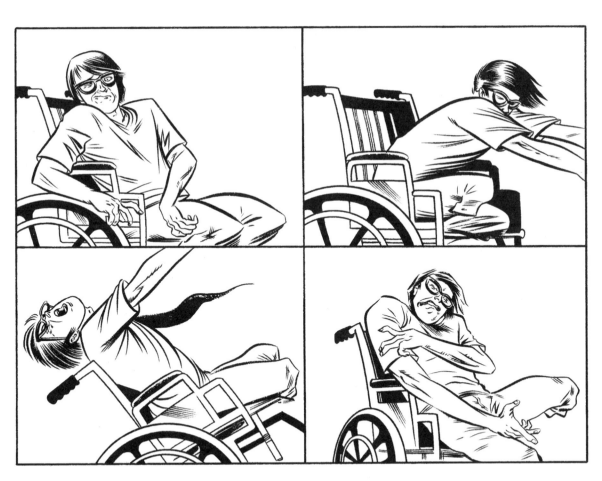

THE HULK RETRIEVES THE BALL, LOOKS BACK UP AT ME WITH THOSE FAR AWAY EYES, CRACKS A TIRED YET GENUINE SMILE, AND TURNS AROUND.

IT DOESN'T MATTER HOW MANY TIMES HE'S GOT TO GO GET THAT BALL OR IF IT TAKES ALL DAY, THAT KID IN THE WHEELCHAIR IS GOING TO GET ONE IN THE HOOP.

THE END.

I'M RIDING MY BICYCLE DOWN CLINTON STREET WHEN I SEE AN AMBULANCE BLOCKING THE MIDDLE OF THE ROAD.

I LOOK TO SEE WHAT THE COPS AND PARAMEDICS ARE LOOKING AT AND IT'S A WELL-DRESSED, WHITE HAIRED OLD LADY

CUDDLED NEXT TO THE BACK WHEEL OF A PARKED CAR

CLUTCHING HER CELL PHONE.

SHE'S BESIDE HERSELF... TRYING TO PUSH THE RIGHT NUMBERS TO REACH HER HUSBAND BUT SHE CAN'T.

I NEED TO CALL MY HUSBAND...

SHE SAYS THIS AS IF SHE NEEDS TO CALL HIM TO SAY GOODBYE.

I NEED TO CALL MY HUSBAND...

I NEED TO CALL MY HUSBAND...

THE PARAMEDIC LEANS IN AND TELLS HER TO CALM DOWN.

EVERYTHING IS GOING TO BE OKAY.

...I NEED TO CALL MY HUSBAND...

THE PARAMEDIC WANTS THE OLD LADY TO HAND OVER HER CELL PHONE SO THEY CAN PULL HER OUT FROM UNDER THE PARKED CAR.

THE OLD LADY WON'T LET GO OF THE PHONE.

SHE NEEDS TO CALL HER HUSBAND ONE LAST TIME.

I FEEL A CHILL CRAWL UP MY SPINE AND IT MAKES ME DIZZY.

I FEEL BAD WATCHING. I CAN'T STAND IT WHEN I CAN'T DO ANYTHING TO HELP, EVEN WHEN PROFESSIONALS ARE DOING THE JOB.

NYC EMS

AS THEY FIGURE OUT A WAY TO PRY HER FROM THE SPACE SHE FELL UNDER, I CYCLE SLOWLY AROUND THE AMBULANCE, SILENTLY WISHING HER WELL.

ON THE OTHER SIDE OF THE AMBULANCE IS A SPORTS CAR WITH TWO SPANISH THUGS DRESSED IN GANG GEAR LOOKING WHITE AS A SHEET.

THEY'RE CLUTCHING THEIR CELL PHONES, TOO.

THEIR EYES ARE GUILTY, FULL OF REMORSE, AND LOCKED IN ON THE OLD LADY'S PLIGHT.

I PUT TWO AND TWO TOGETHER AND REALIZE THAT THEY WERE THE ONES WHO CALLED 911.

I BIKE PAST THE THUG'S SPORTS CAR AND LOOK BACK ONE LAST TIME.

SPLAYED ACROSS THEIR WINDSHIELD IS A ONE WORD DECAL PAINTED HEAVENLY WHITE IN A HIP HOP FONT.

IT SAYS:

BREATHE

THE END.

~CINEMAS~

QUALITY of LIFE ®

IT'S AFTER MIDNIGHT AND I'M RIDING MY BIKE DOWN COURT STREET JUST MINUTES AFTER WATCHING A MOVIE AT MY LOCAL MOVIE THEATER WHEN--

--A COP CAR COMES RACING TOWARDS ME, LIGHTS CONSPICUOUSLY OFF, DOWN THE WRONG SIDE OF A ONE WAY STREET!

I SWERVE TO AVOID SUDDEN IMPACT AND THE POLICE SPEED BY ME WITH NO APOLOGY.

I NOTICE MORE STEALTHY COP CAR ACTION AND KEEP MY EYES LASER FOCUSED ON THE POSSIBILITY OF A CAR CHASE!

NERVOUS, I DECIDE TO RIDE THE EMPTY SIDEWALKS AND CALL MY FRIEND BECAUSE IT'S HIS BIRTHDAY AND I WANT TO BE THE FIRST TO WISH HIM A HAPPY ONE BEFORE I DIE IN A HAIL OF BULLETS.

I CATCH HIM ON THE PHONE AND HE LAUGHS, INFORMING ME HIS TIME ZONE IS AN HOUR EARLIER THAN MINE. HE HAS 45-MINUTES LEFT BEFORE HE TURNS 28.

DRAT!

SUDDENLY, AN UNDERCOVER SQUAD CAR LIGHTS UP BESIDE ME AND THE SHOTGUN COP FLAGS ME TO STOP.

SNAP

I ACCIDENTALLY CLOSE MY CELL PHONE IN MID CONVERSATION AS THE COP CURLS HIS PUDGY FINGERS, SIGNALING ME TO COME CLOSER TO HIS WINDOW.

WHAT'S THE MATTER, OFFICER?

I FIGURE HE WANTS TO KNOW IF I WITNESSED ANY CRIME.

INSTEAD, HE INFORMS ME THAT I'M BREAKING A "QUALITY OF LIFE" LAW RIDING MY BIKE ON THE SIDEWALK.

MY HEAD JERKS AND I LOOK BACK AT HIM LIKE HE'S GOT TO BE KIDDING!

I LOOK DOWN BOTH DIRECTIONS OF THE EMPTY SIDEWALKS AND THERE ARE NO PEOPLE TO BE FOUND AND I SAY AS MUCH.

THE COP DOESN'T CARE. IT'S A PART OF HIS JOB TO ENFORCE THE "QUALITY OF LIFE" IN THIS NEIGHBORHOOD.

HE WANTS MY NAME AND IDENTIFICATION.

I SHOW HIM MY CREDIT CARD BECAUSE MY ONLY I.D., A PASSPORT, IS AT HOME A FEW BLOCKS AWAY.

CHASE
5011 9223 0404 7123
1999 - 07/07 VISA
DEAN HASPIEL

I DIDN'T THINK I NEEDED I.D. TO SEE A MOVIE.

WHAT DO YOU NEED MY NAME FOR?

HE TELLS ME HE'S GOING TO WRITE ME A FINE.

THIS ANGERS ME GREATLY AND I POP MY CELL PHONE OPEN. HE ASKS ME WHO I'M CALLING.

MY LAWYER...

MY RIGHTS THREATEN HIS SHIELD AND HE PUFFS OUT HIS CHEST.

MEANWHILE, HIS PARTNER, THE DRIVER, IGNORES OUR PARLAY WHILE HE CHATS WITH HIS GIRLFRIEND VIA CELL PHONE.

THE COP BACKS DOWN AND SAYS HE WON'T FINE ME BUT THAT HE'LL WRITE ME A SUMMONS TO APPEAR IN COURT SO I CAN EXPLAIN MYSELF TO THE JUDGE.

I LOOK HIM DEAD SQUARE IN HIS BEADY BLACK IRISH EYES AND ASK --

WHY WOULD I WASTE MY TIME DOING SOMETHING LIKE THAT?

HE PULLS OUT THE "QUALITY OF LIFE" CARD HE'S BEEN DANGLING OVER MY HEAD.

YOU COULD RIDE YOUR BIKE AROUND A CORNER --

-- AND HIT A DRUNK STUMBLING OUT OF A BAR, YA KNOW.

YEAH, PROTECT THE INEBRIATED. INCENSED, I TELL HIM THAT I'VE LIVED IN CARROLL GARDENS FOR AWHILE NOW AND I'VE NEVER BEEN CONFRONTED BY SUCH BEHAVIOR.

SNAP

YOU WANT TO KNOW WHAT "QUALITY OF LIFE" IS?

QUALITY OF LIFE IS NOT GETTING KILLED BY A COP CAR SPEEDING DOWN THE WRONG SIDE OF THE STREET --

-- WHILE I, A BICYCLIST WHO HAS THE RIGHT OF WAY, NEARLY GETS HIT!

WHICH IS THE ONLY REASON I ELECTED TO BIKE ON THE EMPTY SIDEWALKS --

-- SO I CAN LIVE!

HIS EYES GLAZE OVER AND HE ADMITS THAT THERE WAS AN INCIDENT A FEW BLOCKS AWAY, MERE MINUTES BEFORE.

I CAN SEE IT IN THE WAY HE SLUMPS BACK AND DEFLATES IN HIS SEAT THAT HE FEELS LIKE A JACKASS.

I GIVE HIM CREDIT FOR CONFIRMING MY STORY.

HE TELLS ME HE'S GOING TO LET ME OFF WITH A VERBAL SLAP AND WARNING.

HIS PARTNER NEVER LOOKS AT ME. HE KNOWS IT'S A BULLCRAP CHARGE.

THEY DRIVE OFF TO FIGHT CRIME AND PROTECT THE INNOCENT.

I CALL MY FRIEND BACK AND WE CHAT UNTIL IT TURNS MIDNIGHT HIS TIME AND I WISH HIM HAPPY BIRTHDAY.

THE END.

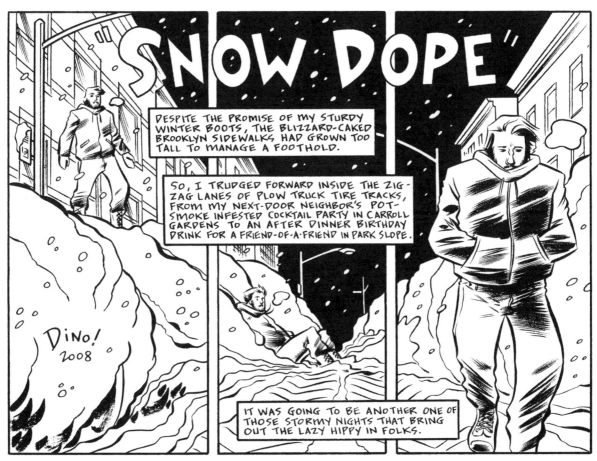

# "SNOW DOPE"

DESPITE THE PROMISE OF MY STURDY WINTER BOOTS, THE BLIZZARD-CAKED BROOKLYN SIDEWALKS HAD GROWN TOO TALL TO MANAGE A FOOTHOLD.

SO, I TRUDGED FORWARD INSIDE THE ZIG-ZAG LANES OF PLOW TRUCK TIRE TRACKS, FROM MY NEXT-DOOR NEIGHBOR'S POT-SMOKE INFESTED COCKTAIL PARTY IN CARROLL GARDENS TO AN AFTER DINNER BIRTHDAY DRINK FOR A FRIEND-OF-A-FRIEND IN PARK SLOPE.

DINO! 2008

IT WAS GOING TO BE ANOTHER ONE OF THOSE STORMY NIGHTS THAT BRING OUT THE LAZY HIPPY IN FOLKS.

MARIJUANA MAKES FOLKS CRIMINALLY SOFT.

PEOPLE WHO NEED WEED TO GET BY ON A SATURDAY NIGHT SHOULD STAY HOME AND WATCH CARTOONS WITH THEIR PALS AND PASS OUT IN MID-MAKE OUT.

OTHERWISE, LEAVE THE NEW YORK CITY NIGHTLIFE TO BRUISERS AND DAMES WHO DRINK THE RYE AND PLAY THE POOL AND DO THE DANCE.

NEVERMIND THE GLASS OF WINE THAT COMPLEMENTS STEAK,

I DRINK TO GET DRUNK.

ALAS, THE PARTIES AFFORDED ME LESS THAN AN HOUR OF BITTERSWEET RELIEF.

I REALIZED THAT IT WAS BETTER TO REJECT ROTE SOCIAL BANTER TO QUELL MY FEAR OF BEING ALONE AND EMBRACE SOLITUDE THIS HOLIDAY WEEKEND.

SO, I NAVIGATED THE NEIGHBORHOODS WITH A PINT OF CHEAP WHISKEY TO KEEP ME WARM AS THE MUFFLED RUMBLING OF AN ELEVATED F-TRAIN SCORED MY MARCH BACK HOME.

THE BLIZZARD'S FROSTY DENOUEMENT WAS TOO DIVINE TO DENY AND I SPENT A SHOCKING AMOUNT OF TIME STARING AT THE FLURRIES OF CRYSTAL SWOOP AROUND ME IN THE CENTER OF AN EERILY QUIET GOWANUS CANAL BRIDGE.

I WAS INTOXICATED ON NATURE...

... AND I DIDN'T WANT TO GO HOME.

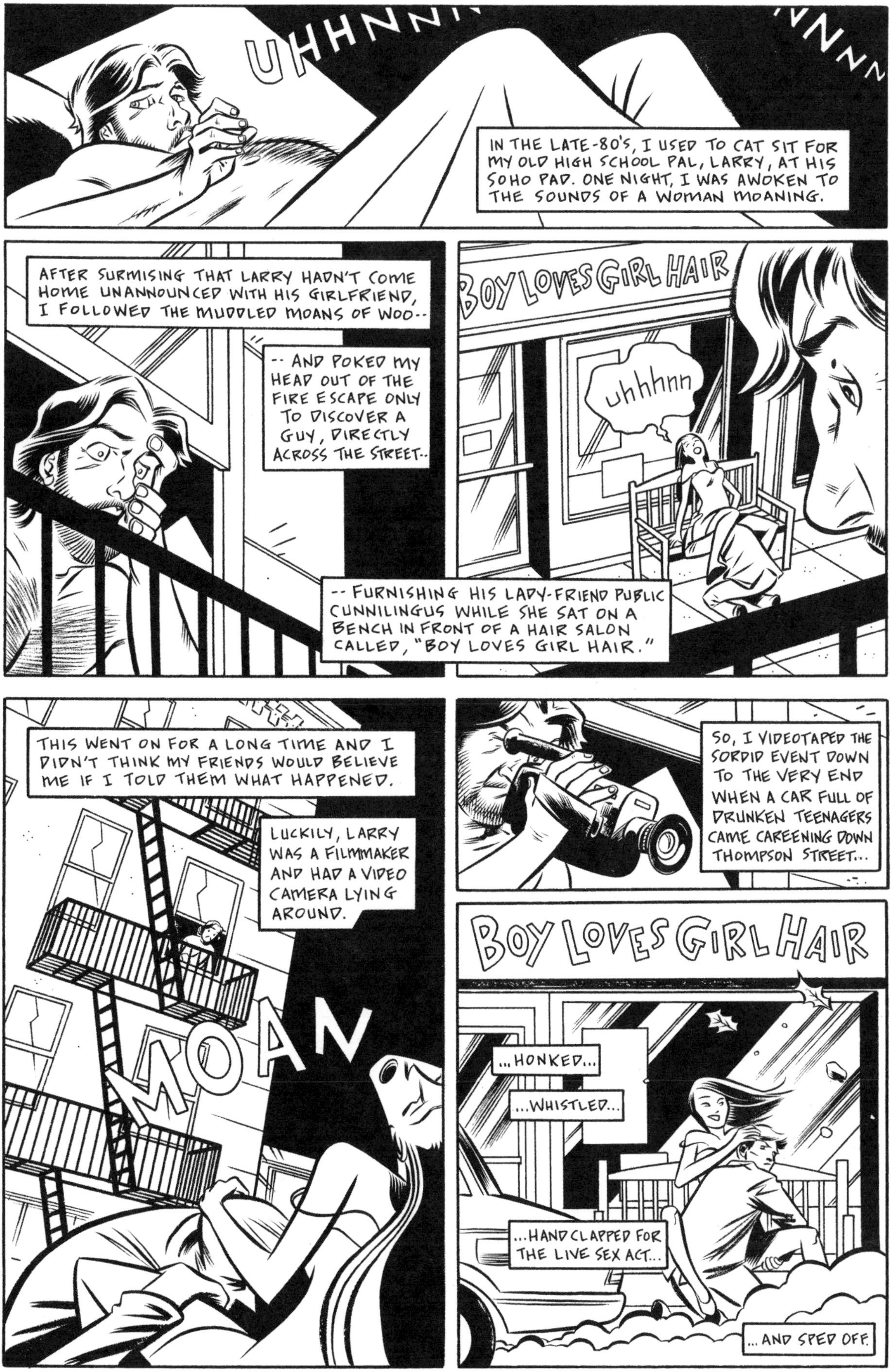
UHHNNN
NNNNN
IN THE LATE-80'S, I USED TO CAT SIT FOR MY OLD HIGH SCHOOL PAL, LARRY, AT HIS SOHO PAD. ONE NIGHT, I WAS AWOKEN TO THE SOUNDS OF A WOMAN MOANING.
AFTER SURMISING THAT LARRY HADN'T COME HOME UNANNOUNCED WITH HIS GIRLFRIEND, I FOLLOWED THE MUDDLED MOANS OF WOO--
-- AND POKED MY HEAD OUT OF THE FIRE ESCAPE ONLY TO DISCOVER A GUY, DIRECTLY ACROSS THE STREET..
BOY LOVES GIRL HAIR
uhhhnn
-- FURNISHING HIS LADY-FRIEND PUBLIC CUNNILINGUS WHILE SHE SAT ON A BENCH IN FRONT OF A HAIR SALON CALLED, "BOY LOVES GIRL HAIR."
THIS WENT ON FOR A LONG TIME AND I DIDN'T THINK MY FRIENDS WOULD BELIEVE ME IF I TOLD THEM WHAT HAPPENED.
LUCKILY, LARRY WAS A FILMMAKER AND HAD A VIDEO CAMERA LYING AROUND.
MOAN
SO, I VIDEOTAPED THE SORDID EVENT DOWN TO THE VERY END WHEN A CAR FULL OF DRUNKEN TEENAGERS CAME CAREENING DOWN THOMPSON STREET...
BOY LOVES GIRL HAIR
...HONKED...
...WHISTLED...
...HAND CLAPPED FOR THE LIVE SEX ACT...
...AND SPED OFF.

FOR SOME REASON, THIS DISPLAY OF CELEBRATION RANKLED THE MAN AND HE PICKED UP THE HEAVY BENCH THAT HIS PARAMOUR WAS SITTING ON, DRAGGED IT ACROSS THE STREET...

...AND DUMPED IT INTO A PILE OF GARBAGE.

SKREEEEETCH

THE SELF-ENTITLED LOVERS HURRIED OFF IN A SCURRY AND THE AMATEUR PORNO VIDEO BECAME A FUNNY STAG FILM TO SHOW AT PARTIES.

A YEAR LATER, I MOVED INTO LARRY'S APARTMENT AND BEFRIENDED, SERGE, THE GAY OWNER OF 'BOY LOVES GIRL HAIR.'

SERGE WOULD BREW ME FRESH ESPRESSO AND COMPLAIN ABOUT ALL THE RATS AND THIEVES IN THE NEIGHBORHOOD. I FINALLY BUILT UP THE COURAGE TO CONFIRM SERGE'S RAGE.

DID YOU EVER WONDER WHAT HAPPENED TO YOUR BENCH?

HE GAVE ME A LOOK.

SO, I SHOWED SERGE THE INFAMOUS VIDEO I SHOT AND HIS JAW DROPPED.

A WEEK LATER, I SPOTTED A FEMALE EXHIBITIONIST ACROSS THE STREET.

SHE LIVED ABOVE 'BOY LOVES GIRL HAIR' AND WOULD HAVE SEX WITH HER BOYFRIEND IN THE WINDOW. HE WAS MISSING A FOOT.

NEVER TOO SHY TO CALL SOMEONE OUT ON HIS OR HER SHENANIGANS, I EVENTUALLY BEFRIENDED THE EXHIBITIONIST AND WE SHOUTED OUR TELEPHONE NUMBERS ALOUD.

Hi.

Hi.

HER NAME WAS AMY AND SHE RAN A WRITER'S ROOM IN THE WEST VILLAGE.

ONE TIME, AMY CALLED AND ASKED ME TO VIDEO-TAPE HER WHILE SHE GROOMED HER NETHER REGIONS IN THE WINDOW WITH A LARGE PAIR OF SCISSORS I'D PREVIOUSLY LENT HER.

THE WORD 'FEAR' WAS INSCRIBED ON ONE OF THE BLADES AS SHE SPRINKLED FRESHLY TRIMMED PUBIC HAIR UPON THE 'BOY LOVES GIRL HAIR' SIGN.

MY DOCUMENTATION OF AMY WAS SCRATCHING A MUTUAL, UNORTHODOX, INTERACTIVE ITCH.

WHEN I WAS STILL A TEENAGER, MY FATHER CAME HOME REALLY LATE ONE NIGHT AND WARNED ME --

THERE ARE THINGS YOU WOULD NEVER EVER CONSIDER DOING... ...BEFORE MIDNIGHT.

SPRINKLES OF ANGEL HAIR TURNED INTO WHITE CRYSTALS OF SNOW WHEN WINTER CAME.

DAD HAD A LOOK ON HIS FACE THAT SUGGESTED SOMETHING HAD GONE WRONG. OR, RIGHT.

NO MATTER, AMY AND I SHARED A BIZARRE YET PURELY PLATONIC PARLAY.

AMY AND I REPAIRED TO THE NEARBY STREETS OF TRIBECA WHILE SHE DANCED NAKED IN THE SNOW AND I TOOK PROVOCATIVE PICTURES WITH MY CANDID CAMERA.

AMY EVENTUALLY BROKE UP WITH HER ONE-FOOTED BOYFRIEND AND SOON HAD ANOTHER MAN WHO BRANDISHED A MAGNIFICENT, AQUILINE NOSE BUT INSISTED ON MAKING LOVE WITH THE SHADES PULLED DOWN.

A YEAR LATER, I MOVED IN WITH MY THEN-GIRLFRIEND WHO LIVED IN ALPHABET CITY AND I NEVER SAW AMY AGAIN.

BUYER BEWARE

IT WAS 4AM ON A SATURDAY NIGHT AND MY DRUNKEN MASS WAS INSTANTLY SOBERED BY THE HORRIFIC SOUNDS OF A LOUD SMASH FOLLOWED BY THE SHOWER OF BROKEN GLASS EXPLODING.

A MOMENT LATER I HEARD A PERSON CRYING WHILE DRAGGING THINGS UP AND DOWN THE COMMUNAL STAIRWELL OF MY APARTMENT BUILDING.

A HANGOVER WAS ABOUT TO BE BORN 12-HOURS EARLIER THAN SCHEDULED.

I HEARD THE METAL DOOR OF MY APARTMENT BUILDING CLANG OPEN AND I RAN TO MY FIRE ESCAPE WINDOW TO WITNESS THE CULPRIT.

MOTHER DOG.

INSTEAD, I SAW PILLOWS AND CLOTHES AND BAGS OF STUFF STREWN ABOUT THE STREET.

THERE WAS A LOUD STOMPING NOISE IN THE STAIRWELL, SO, I TIPTOED TO MY FRONT DOOR AND HOVERED BY THE PEEPHOLE TO SEE WHO WAS FREAKING OUT—

—AND SAW A GIANT MAN CRYING AND CARRYING A BROKEN MIRROR DOWN THE STAIRS.

I SLOWLY UNLOCKED MY DOOR AND LOOKED AT THE DAMAGE HE'D MADE IN OUR HALLWAY.

THE LIGHT BULB WAS SWINGING AND FLICKERING ON AND OFF LIKE AT THE END OF ALFRED HITCHCOCK'S PSYCHO, AND THERE WERE SHARDS OF GLASS ON THE TILE FLOOR.

I DECIDED TO VENTURE DOWN THE STAIRS AND WAS MET WITH THE CARNAGE OF WALL SCRAPES AND BROKEN THINGS.

I COULD HEAR THE GIANT MAN COMING BACK UP THE STAIRS. SO, I DIPPED INTO THE SAFETY ZONE OF MY HOME UNTIL I COULD ASCERTAIN WHERE HE WAS GOING --

-- WHICH TURNED OUT TO BE RIGHT NEXT DOOR.

THE GIANT MAN WAS JOHN, MY NEXT-DOOR NEIGHBOR WHO WAS SIX-FOOT, FOUR INCHES TALL, HANDSOME AND GAY.

JOHN WORKED IN FASHION AND WAS ALWAYS EXTREMELY FRIENDLY AND NICE.

POOPIE-BOPS LIKES DRY FOOD MIXED IN WITH HER WET FOOD TWICE A DAY.

JOHN ASKED ME TO TAKE CARE OF HIS CAT WHENEVER HE WENT ON VACATION TO TURKS AND CAICOS AND, WITH GOOD HISTORY BETWEEN US --

-- I DECIDED TO CONFRONT JOHN'S RAMPAGE.

THE WOODEN FLOORS WERE COVERED IN BROKEN GLASS AND CERAMIC AND JOHN'S CAT JOGGED DOWN THE HALL AND HID UNDER A BED.

THE INTERCOM'S WALL WAS SHREDDED DOWN TO THE FENCED IN GUTS AND WIRES.

A LARGE SCRAPING TOOL SAT IN A MOUND OF A THOUSAND PAINT CHIPS.

I GRIPPED MYSELF AND CALLED HIS NAME.

JOHN?

HE LOOKED AT ME WITH TEARS IN HIS EYES LIKE A DESPERATE MAN CLINGING TO THE END OF HIS ROPE.

I WAS NO LONGER SCARED OF HIS RAMPAGE AND, INSTEAD, I FELT BAD FOR THE GUY.

I SAT JOHN DOWN ON HIS COUCH AND GOT HIM A PLASTIC CUP OF WATER IN CASE HE DECIDED TO BREAK THAT, TOO.

HE STARTED TO WEEP EVEN HARDER THAN BEFORE. HE DELIBERATED HIS MORTALITY AND CRIED --

IT'S OVER. IT'S ALL OVER.

I HAD NEVER SEEN A MAN LOOK MORE ALONE.

I CONSOLED JOHN FOR A GOOD TWENTY-MINUTES WHEN, LIKE NINJAS, A FEW POLICEMEN APPEARED BEHIND US, WINKING AND STIFLING CHUCKLES --

--LIKE THEY'D BUSTED US FOR HAVING A KNOCK DOWN, DRAG OUT, LOVERS QUARREL AND WERE ABOUT TO ENGAGE MAKE-UP SEX.

43

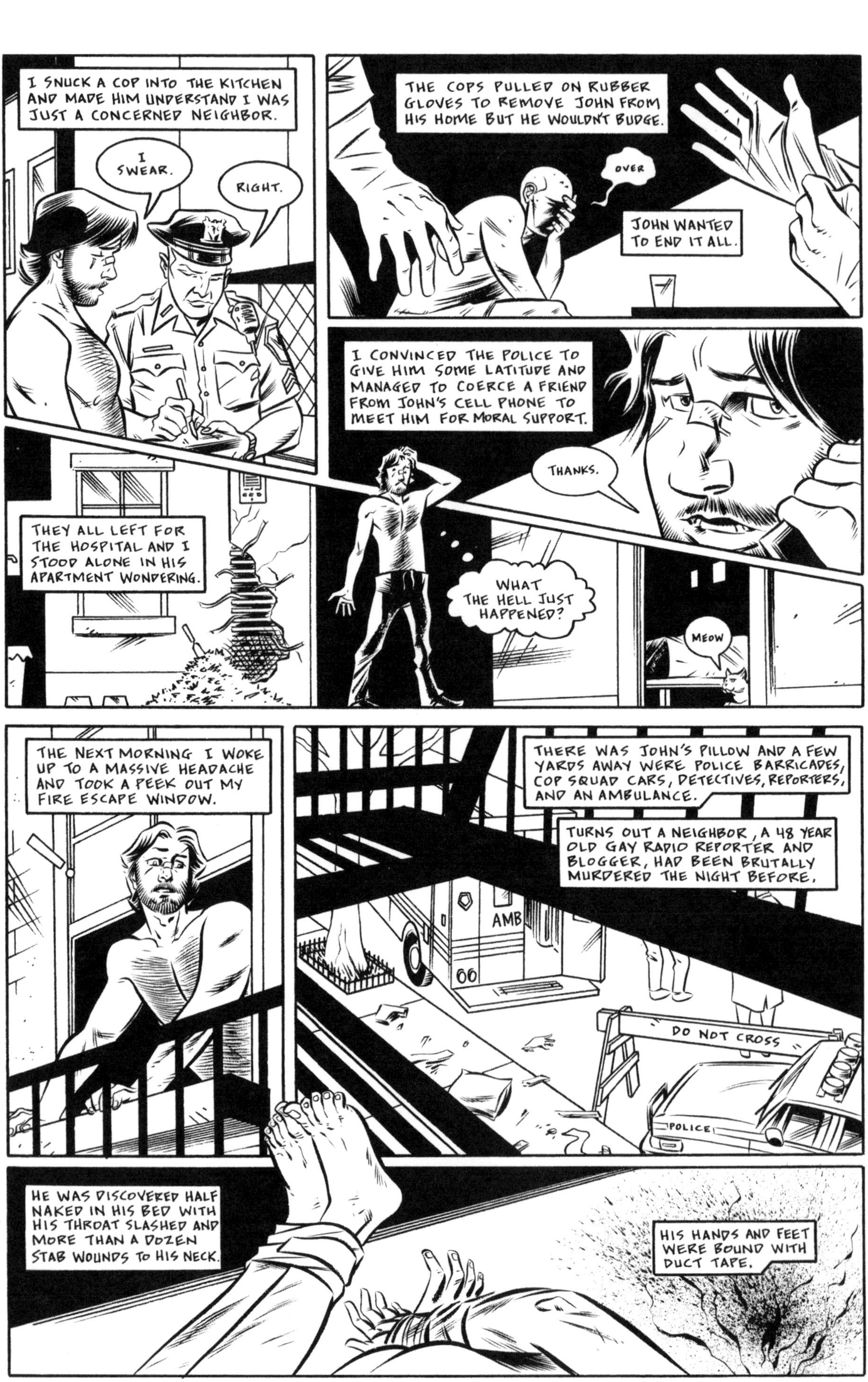
I SNUCK A COP INTO THE KITCHEN AND MADE HIM UNDERSTAND I WAS JUST A CONCERNED NEIGHBOR.
I SWEAR.
RIGHT.
THE COPS PULLED ON RUBBER GLOVES TO REMOVE JOHN FROM HIS HOME BUT HE WOULDN'T BUDGE.
OVER
JOHN WANTED TO END IT ALL.
I CONVINCED THE POLICE TO GIVE HIM SOME LATITUDE AND MANAGED TO COERCE A FRIEND FROM JOHN'S CELL PHONE TO MEET HIM FOR MORAL SUPPORT.
THANKS.
THEY ALL LEFT FOR THE HOSPITAL AND I STOOD ALONE IN HIS APARTMENT WONDERING.
WHAT THE HELL JUST HAPPENED?
MEOW
THE NEXT MORNING I WOKE UP TO A MASSIVE HEADACHE AND TOOK A PEEK OUT MY FIRE ESCAPE WINDOW.
THERE WAS JOHN'S PILLOW AND A FEW YARDS AWAY WERE POLICE BARRICADES, COP SQUAD CARS, DETECTIVES, REPORTERS, AND AN AMBULANCE.
TURNS OUT A NEIGHBOR, A 48 YEAR OLD GAY RADIO REPORTER AND BLOGGER, HAD BEEN BRUTALLY MURDERED THE NIGHT BEFORE.
AMB
66
DO NOT CROSS
POLICE
HE WAS DISCOVERED HALF NAKED IN HIS BED WITH HIS THROAT SLASHED AND MORE THAN A DOZEN STAB WOUNDS TO HIS NECK.
HIS HANDS AND FEET WERE BOUND WITH DUCT TAPE.

HAD JOHN'S MELTDOWN BEEN A RUSE, A REACTION TO MURDER?

I KNOCKED ON JOHN'S DOOR AND IT CREAKED OPEN.

THERE WAS STILL DAMAGE EVERYWHERE AND HIS CAT WAS HIDING UNDER THE BED.

I MADE SURE THERE WAS PLENTY OF FOOD AND WATER FOR THE ABANDONED PET AND CLOSED THE DOOR.

HAD MY HEROIC BEHAVIOR GIVEN JOHN SOME SORT OF TWISTED ALIBI?

THE NEXT DAY, I KNOCKED ON JOHN'S DOOR, AGAIN, BUT IT WAS LOCKED AND IT APPEARED THAT NO ONE WAS HOME.

A WEEK LATER, I RECEIVED A HAND-WRITTEN NOTE FROM JOHN THANKING ME FOR SAVING HIS LIFE.

JACK

THE NEXT MORNING, NEWS BROKE THAT POLICE ARRESTED A TEENAGE IMMIGRANT FOR THE MURDER OF MY NEARBY NEIGHBOR.

TURNS OUT THE RADIO REPORTER/BLOGGER HAD PUT AN AD ONLINE SOLICITING A STRANGER FOR ROUGH SEX.

HE PAID THE STRANGER $50 TO BE DISCIPLINED, ONLY THE KID BROUGHT A REAL KNIFE TO A CHARADE.

YOU GET WHAT YOU PAY FOR.

# THE BEAUTIFUL GIRL WITH BOLSHEVIK BREASTS

YEARS AGO, I DATED A GORGEOUS POLISH/RUSSIAN GIRL NAMED ELEKTRA WHO INSISTED ON RIPPING OFF HER SHIRT AND BRA THE MINUTE SHE CAME HOME FROM WORK.

SHE HAD BEAUTIFUL BREASTS AND, IF SHE FELT CONFINED AND NEEDED TO BARE HER WARES, WHO WAS I TO KNOCK HER?

MY LIVING ROOM HAS WINDOWS THAT FACE THE STREET.

"FREEDOM. YOU'VE GOTTA GIVE FOR WHAT YOU TAKE." ♪

ELEKTRA LOVED TO SING AND SHE WOULD HOLD A PHANTOM MICROPHONE IN HER HAND AND CROON TO THE SONGS OF GEORGE MICHAEL AND BJORK WHILE DANCING TOPLESS IN THE LIVING ROOM.

♪ "I'M GOING HUNTING. I'M THE HUNTER." ♪

SHE WAS MORE FUN THAN HORROR MOVIES AND A BOTTLE OF BOURBON.

ONE EVENING, WHILE OGLING ELEKTRA'S BOBBING NIPPLES AS SHE PERFORMED HER ONE-WOMAN CONCERT CUM STRIP TEASE --

-- MY EYES CAUGHT AN ACT OF SHADY STEALTH.

I DISCOVERED AN OLD MAN FROM ACROSS THE STREET STARING IN AWE FROM HIS WINDOW AND I ALERTED ELEKTRA OF HER NEWFOUND BOYFRIEND.

SHE FACED THE NEIGHBOR WITH FULL FRONTAL FLAIR AND BEGAN TO SING GEORGE MICHAEL'S "I WANT YOUR SEX."

SHE HAD A GREAT SENSE OF HUMOR BUT THE OLD MAN WAS SHY AS HE PULLED HIS SHADE BACK ASHAMED OF GETTING BUSTED FOR HIS APPRECIATION.

CURTAINS RIPPLED SEVERAL TIMES AS THE OLD MAN STOLE SNEAK PEAKS FROM WITHIN THE DARK.

I REALIZED MY ORCHESTRA SEAT WAS FAR SUPERIOR TO THE OLD MAN'S BLEACHER SEAT AND EVENTUALLY IGNORED HIM TO INDULGE MY GIRLFRIEND.

TWENTY MINUTES LATER, ELEKTRA AND I WERE LAUGHING ABOUT THE INCIDENT WHEN --

?

--I NOTICED BURSTS OF RED AND BLUE LIGHT BOUNCING OFF HER BREASTS.

47

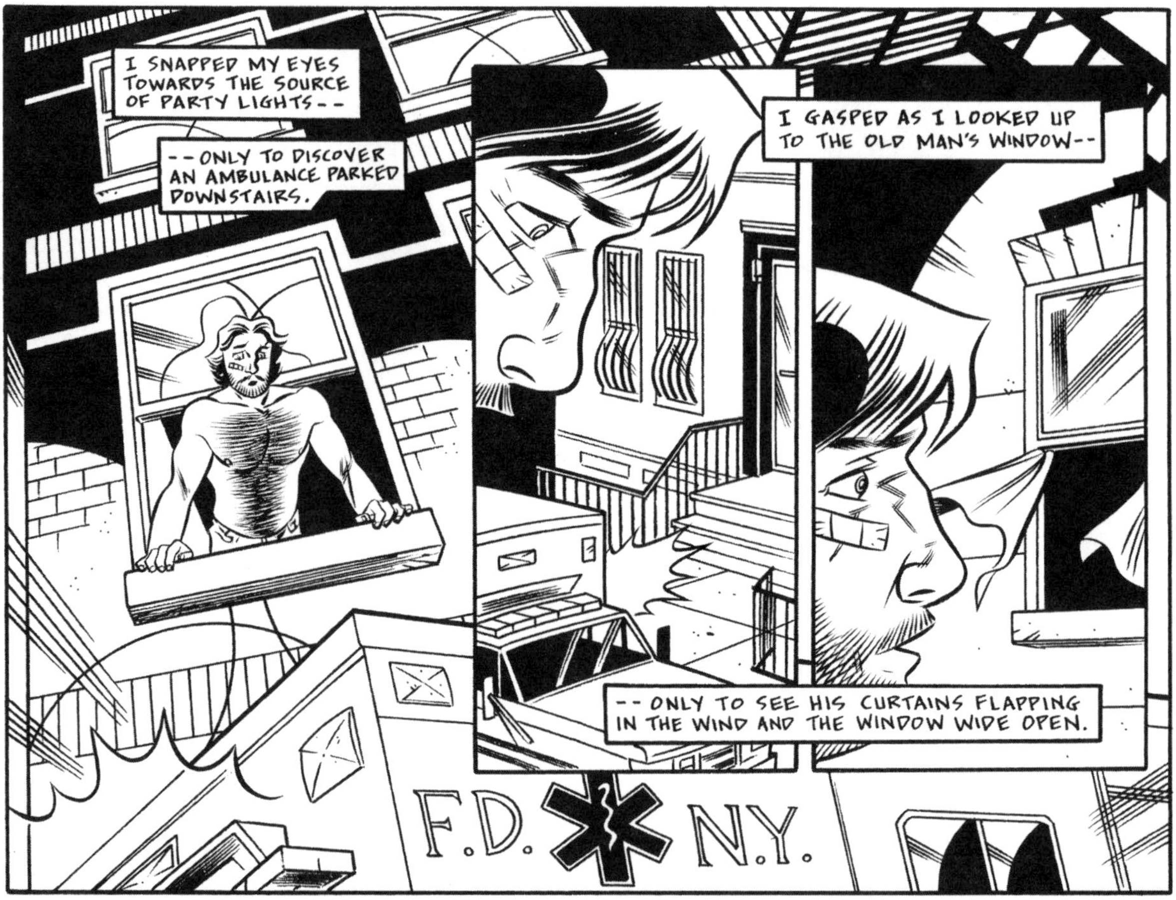
I SNAPPED MY EYES TOWARDS THE SOURCE OF PARTY LIGHTS--
--ONLY TO DISCOVER AN AMBULANCE PARKED DOWNSTAIRS.
I GASPED AS I LOOKED UP TO THE OLD MAN'S WINDOW--
--ONLY TO SEE HIS CURTAINS FLAPPING IN THE WIND AND THE WINDOW WIDE OPEN.
F.D. N.Y.

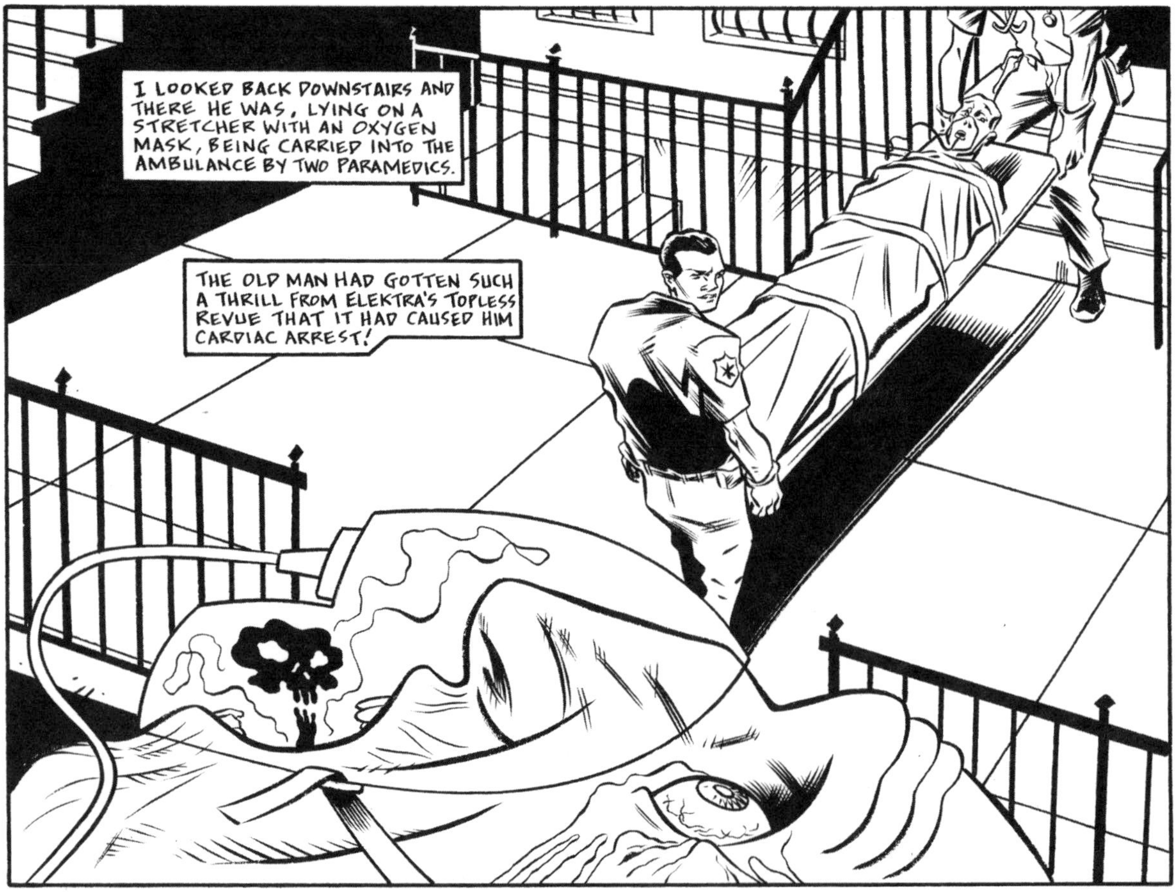
I LOOKED BACK DOWNSTAIRS AND THERE HE WAS, LYING ON A STRETCHER WITH AN OXYGEN MASK, BEING CARRIED INTO THE AMBULANCE BY TWO PARAMEDICS.
THE OLD MAN HAD GOTTEN SUCH A THRILL FROM ELEKTRA'S TOPLESS REVUE THAT IT HAD CAUSED HIM CARDIAC ARREST!

TO BE HONEST, ELEKTRA WAS FLATTERED THAT HER BREASTS COULD CAUSE SUCH A LIFE THREATENING REACTION BUT FELT BAD FOR THE OLD MAN BECAUSE HE NEVER RETURNED HOME.

A FEW MONTHS LATER, ELEKTRA DROPPED THE DREADED H-BOMB ON ME AND DECLARED MY BUDDING ART CAREER A "HOBBY"...

--AND WONDERED WHEN I'D "GET A REAL JOB?"

DESPITE HER DESIRE TO PERFORM, ELEKTRA WAS A PRACTICAL GIRL WHO WORKED IN FINANCE AND PREFERRED SECURITY TO RISK.

"IT RUBS LOTION ON ITS SKIN OR ELSE IT GETS THE HOSE AGAIN."

ALAS, OUR PHILOSOPHICAL DIFFERENCES LED US TO DISBANDING AND I WAS NO LONGER THE RECIPIENT OF NUDE, HAPPY HOUR KARAOKE IN MY LIVING ROOM.

# "DUMBO"

MAYBE IT'S BECAUSE I LOOK ORNERY.

OR, MAYBE I LOOK LIKE THE KIND OF GUY WHO COULD ROB SOMEBODY.

WHATEVER.

IT WAS A NICE DAY TO SHOOT A MOVIE AND MY OLD COLLEGE FILM CLASS-MATE, SAUL, ASKED ME TO ACT LIKE A THIEF IN HIS FILM, "SABOTAGED."

THE

THE LOCATION WAS SET IN D.U.M.B.O. (DOWN UNDER THE MANHATTAN BRIDGE OVERPASS) AND I WAS TO WEAR ALL BLACK AND STEAL A PURSE FROM A LADY AND GET BUSTED BY A SUPERHERO.

SIMPLE ENOUGH.

THE WAY WE REHEARSED IT WAS: SAUL'S MOM STARTS WALKING AND I COME RUSHING OUT OF NOWHERE AND SNATCH HER PURSE.

SUDDENLY, A SUPERHERO DRESSED IN FULL CAPE AND MASK COSTUME, COMES AFTER ME AND SHOUTS --

STOP! THIEF!

--WHICH, AS DIRECTED, PROMPTS ME TO FLASH HIM THE HAIRY EYEBALL BEFORE RUNNING DOWN THE BLOCK AND OFF-CAMERA.

SAUL'S CATALYTIC SIREN OF "ACTION!" LAUNCHES HIS MOTHER'S OBLIVIOUS DAWDLING, WHICH PROMPTS MY STEALTHY DESCENT AS I GRAB HER PURSE AND SPRINT DOWN THE BLOCK.

THE SUPERHERO SCREAMS...

CAR!

--AND I TURN MY FACE TOWARDS HIM TO SNEER, THINKING HE SAID, "STOP! THIEF!" WHEN, SUDDENLY--

--A FOUR-WHEELED METAL MONSTER COMES RAMMING INTO ME, FULL THROTTLE, PRACTICALLY CRUSHING MY LEGS INTO A BUILDING.

I TRY TO HALT MY ASCENT AND, INSTEAD, SMASHED MY ENTIRE LEFT SIDE INTO THE BACK OF THE VEHICLE, FLIPPING OVER ITS HOOD AND CRASHING INTO THE SIDEWALK BELOW.

WITHIN SECONDS I STOOD UP IN SHOCK, COMPLETELY CONFUSED.

WHERE HAD THE CAR COME FROM? WHY DID IT RUN INTO ME?

THIS WASN'T IN THE REHEARSAL.

I WAS REELING.

EVERYBODY CAME RUSHING TO MY AID AS I STUMBLED, FEELING THE PAIN COMPETE WITH MY ADRENALINE RUSH, SEIZING MY MUSCLES.

THE DRIVER, A DIRTY BLONDE BOHEMIAN, HAD THE LOOK OF FEAR IN HIS BIG BLACK EYES!

HE THOUGHT I WAS ACTUALLY SNATCHING THE POOR LADIES PURSE, MISTAKING ME FOR A REAL THIEF, AND WENT BATMAN ON ME WITH HIS HATCHBACK.

BUT.-

HE CLAIMED THAT A CRIMINAL HAD STOLEN SOME LADIES PURSE THE WEEK BEFORE AND FIGURED I WAS THE CULPRIT, NEVER ONCE NOTICING A CAMERA CREW OR A LIFE-SIZED SUPERHERO CHASING AFTER ME!

TOO DAZED TO FULLY CONSIDER HIS VIGILANTE ACT, I WAS SEEING STARS AND PLAYING MEDIC ON MYSELF.

OUCH.

MY LEFT THIGH WAS SMARTING FROM THE PUNCH OF THE CAR AND MY FOOT WAS BURNING FROM BLUE FLAMES OF PAIN.

MY LEFT WRIST AND FOREARM WAS GIVING ME THE MOST TROUBLE AS MOLTEN HOT SPLINTERS RAKED AT MY TENDONS.

LIGAMENTS SCREAMED FROM NUGGETS OF NAPALM AND MY HEAD WAS DIZZY FROM NAUSEA.

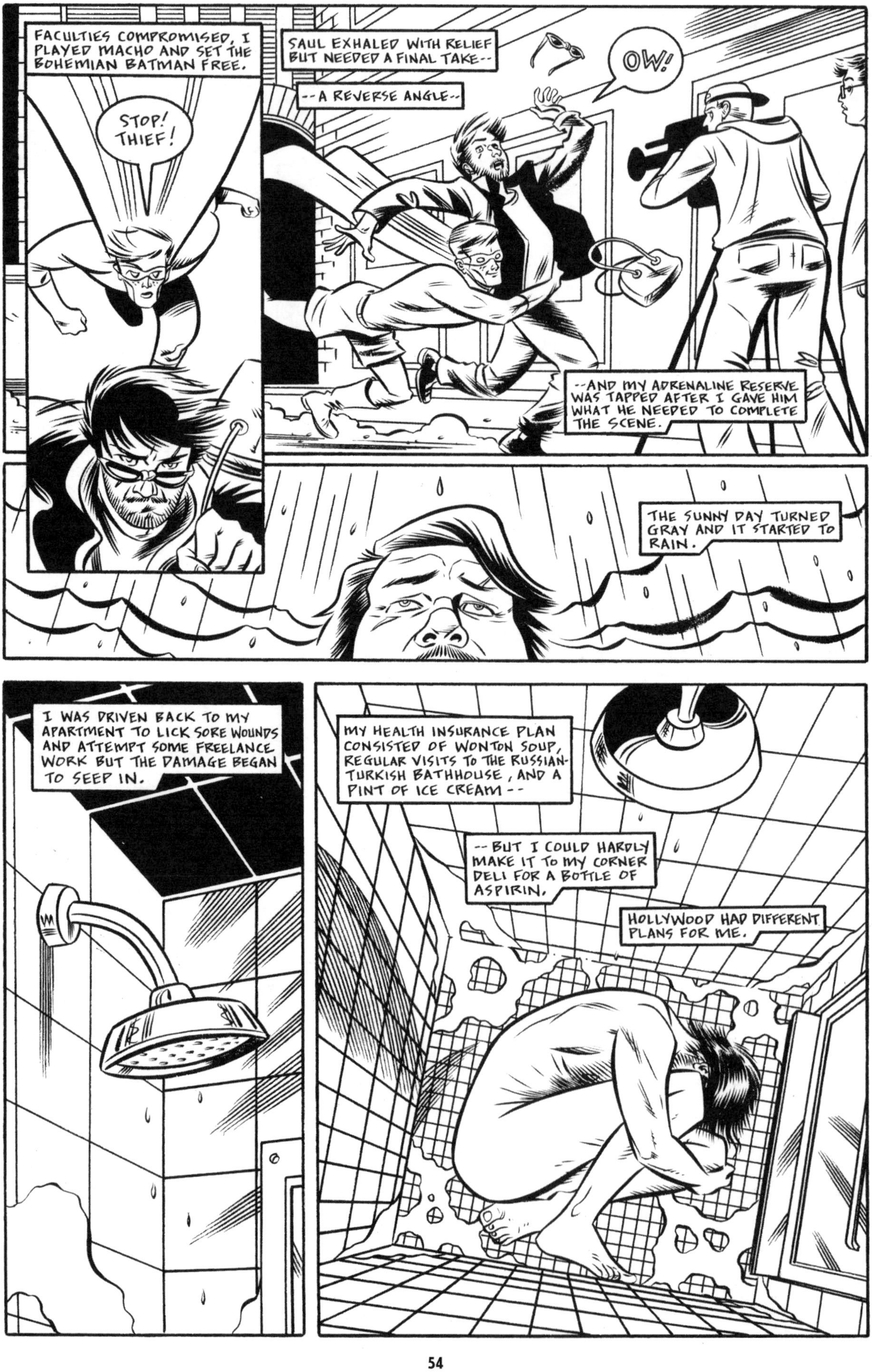
FACULTIES COMPROMISED, I PLAYED MACHO AND SET THE BOHEMIAN BATMAN FREE.
STOP! THIEF!
SAUL EXHALED WITH RELIEF BUT NEEDED A FINAL TAKE--
--A REVERSE ANGLE--
OW!
--AND MY ADRENALINE RESERVE WAS TAPPED AFTER I GAVE HIM WHAT HE NEEDED TO COMPLETE THE SCENE.
THE SUNNY DAY TURNED GRAY AND IT STARTED TO RAIN.
I WAS DRIVEN BACK TO MY APARTMENT TO LICK SORE WOUNDS AND ATTEMPT SOME FREELANCE WORK BUT THE DAMAGE BEGAN TO SEEP IN.
MY HEALTH INSURANCE PLAN CONSISTED OF WONTON SOUP, REGULAR VISITS TO THE RUSSIAN-TURKISH BATHHOUSE, AND A PINT OF ICE CREAM--
--BUT I COULD HARDLY MAKE IT TO MY CORNER DELI FOR A BOTTLE OF ASPIRIN.
HOLLYWOOD HAD DIFFERENT PLANS FOR ME.

NO, YOU BROUGHT TWO TOO MANY.

BEEF WITH TOMATO

BZZT

BZT

HUH?

BZT

GUHHH

RNHHN

A ZOMBIE APOCALYPSE WAS THE FIRST THOUGHT THAT OCCUPIED MY MIND WHEN THE BLACKOUT HAPPENED.

CHALK IT UP TO READING TOO MANY JACK KIRBY AND JOHNNY CRAIG MONSTER COMIC BOOKS AND ENJOYING TOO MANY LATE NIGHT HAMMER HORROR MOVIES --

--BUT, ONCE MY BRAIN SETTLED, IT WAS THE POST-TRAUMATIC STRESS DISORDER BLUES THAT KICKED IN--

HUCHHK

-- AND THE SOBERING REALITY CHECK THAT NORMAL PEOPLE COULD WREAK WORSE HAVOC THAN AN UPRISING OF THE DEAD.

I QUICKLY SURMISED THAT, DURING DESPERATE TIMES, ONE COULD NEGOTIATE FRIENDS AND FAMILY BUT A STRANGER IN NEED WOULD TEST THE VERY NATURE AND ENDURANCE OF HUMANITY.

EVER SINCE THE TRAGIC EVENTS OF 9/11 AND THE ENSUING WAR THEREAFTER, EVERYBODY WAS WALKING ON EGG-SHELLS, WAITING FOR THE PROVERBIAL "OTHER SHOE" TO DROP...

...AND I WAS REMINDED BY MANKIND'S INNATE BEHAVIOR THAT WE'RE TRAINED TO PRACTICE COURTESY AND TAUGHT GOOD MANNERS BUT, WHEN PUSH COMES TO SHOVE--

--WE'RE ALL TEETERING ON THE EDGE OF SLIPPING BACKWARDS INTO THE SAVAGE RESOLVE OF OUR NEANDERTHAL ANCESTORS.

AND, WHEN THE GOING GETS ROUGH, THE ROUGH GETS PRIMAL WITH A BOOSTER SHOT OF RAW ADRENALINE AND ANYTHING YOUR FISTS CAN MAKE MULCH WITH.

THUS, WERE THE PANICKED FEELINGS PROMPTED BY THE NORTHEAST BLACKOUT OF 2003, A MASSIVE WIDESPREAD OUTAGE, AFFECTING OVER 55 MILLION PEOPLE DURING THE LATE AFTERNOON OF A MID-AUGUST DAY.

COUGH!

LUCKILY, NOXIOUS FUMES BILLOWING FROM THE WINDOW BROKE MY NEUROTIC SPELL AS I HEARD RANTS AND RAVES CRYING A COMMUNAL FOUL ON THE STREET BELOW.

COUGH COUGH

MY OBNOXIOUS NEIGHBOR, A WEALTHY ARCHITECT PROTECTED BY HIS GATED CARRIAGE HOUSE, INSISTED ON BEING THE ONLY RESIDENT TO ENJOY ELECTRICITY WHILE THE REST OF US PLUGGED OUR COLLECTIVE OLFACTORY FROM THE LOUD NOISE AND RANCID POLLUTION HIS GENERATOR EMITTED.

THANKFULLY, MY FEARS OF A CATACLYSMIC ZOMBIE MASSACRE WERE TEMPORARILY STIFLED WHEN UNANSWERED QUESTIONS TO A SUDDEN BLACKOUT HAD AN INTERIM VILLAIN TO POINT OUR FINGERS AT.

DESPITE THE RELIEF OF AN AD HOC BAD GUY, DUSK WAS STARTING TO SETTLE AND CANDLES AND BATTERIES WERE RAPIDLY BECOMING SCARCE, ALBEIT HIGH-COST ITEMS.

WHO KNEW HOW LONG THIS BLACKOUT WAS GOING TO LAST?

POTS OF SPAGHETTI WERE COOKED AND CONSUMED BY MY NEIGHBORS AS WE CAUGHT UP WITH EACH OTHER'S LIVES AND LISTENED TO MY RADIO FOR STATUS REPORTS.

ALAS, IT WAS THE SUMMER HEAT AND A MASS DELUGE OF CRANKED UP AIR CONDITIONING UNITS THAT COMPROMISED THE SYSTEM AND LEFT US IN THE DARK.

RING

FOR SOME REASON, LANDLINES WERE FUNCTIONING, AND AN UNEXPECTED PHONE CALL FROM MY EX-GIRLFRIEND INTERRUPTED THE NEIGHBORLY PARLEY AND HER TENDER VOICE CAUSED ME CONCERN.

I'LL BE THERE AS SOON AS I CAN.

SHE DIDN'T SOUND SCARED BUT I KNEW THAT IF MY EX-GIRLFRIEND CALLED ME, IT MEANT SOMETHING WAS AWRY.

THE NEAR-BLIND BIKE RIDE PROMPTED PARANOIA OF GETTING ATTACKED BY THUGS AND LOOTERS BEFORE I COULD COMPLETE MY SERPENTINE TREK BETWEEN CARROLL GARDENS AND PARK SLOPE.

THE CITY HAD LOST ITS OMNISCIENT HUM AND THE EERIE QUIET CONTRASTED WITH THE PITTER-PATTER OF VANDAL FEET SPARKED THOUGHTS OF MORTALITY AS I PONDERED MY PREMATURE DEMISE.

A GIRL'S ASS.

"HOW DO YOU THINK YOU'RE GOING TO DIE?" A QUESTION I'D NEVER FULLY CONSIDERED UNTIL TODAY.

AND, MY FIRST AND ONLY ANSWER WAS--

A GIRL'S ASS.

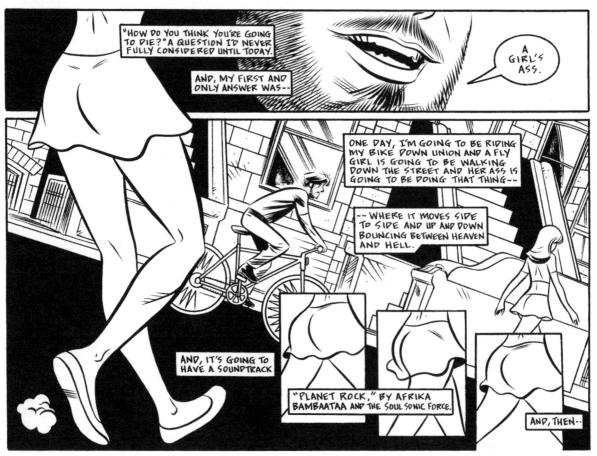

AND, IT'S GOING TO HAVE A SOUNDTRACK

ONE DAY, I'M GOING TO BE RIDING MY BIKE DOWN UNION AND A FLY GIRL IS GOING TO BE WALKING DOWN THE STREET AND HER ASS IS GOING TO BE DOING THAT THING--

--WHERE IT MOVES SIDE TO SIDE AND UP AND DOWN BOUNCING BETWEEN HEAVEN AND HELL.

"PLANET ROCK," BY AFRIKA BAMBAATAA AND THE SOUL SONIC FORCE.

AND, THEN--

IT'LL BE OVER, JUST LIKE THAT, AND I'LL BE DEAD. CRUSHED BY A CAR I NEVER SAW COMING.

WHEN I FINALLY ARRIVED TO THE FAR SIDE OF PARK SLOPE, MY EX-GIRLFRIEND WAS HAPPY AND DRUNK.

HER NEIGHBORS HAD SAFELY QUARANTINED THEIR BROWNSTONE UTOPIA WITH MINI-CAMPFIRE SITES AND EVERYONE HAD PULLED OUT THEIR SECRET STASHES OF HOOCH LIKE A SPEAKEASY INSPIRED BLOCK PARTY.

I WAS HANDED A GLASS OF WHISKEY AND ENCOURAGED TO SING SONGS WHILE PEOPLE ROASTED MARSHMALLOWS AND SHARED THEIR FAVORITE NEW YORK STORIES.

I THOUGHT ABOUT MY PERSONAL HISTORY WITH THE BOROUGHS AND PONDERED THE PERFECT NYC DAY.

THERE IS THE NEW YORK CITY THAT TOURISTS VISIT AND THEN THERE IS THE NYC THAT NATIVES PARTAKE IN AND KEEP ON THE DOWN LOW.

LIKE A JACKIE GLEASON HONEYMOONERS RE-RUN OR AN ISSUE OF THE FANTASTIC FOUR THAT COMES OUT EVERY MONTH SINCE BEFORE YOU WERE BORN...

...THERE ARE PLACES IN THE CITY YOU CAN ALWAYS COUNT ON BEING THERE.

WO-HOP 和合 RESTAURANT

WO-HOP

BEEF WITH TOMATO OVER WHITE RICE?

WITH HOT AND SOUR SOUP AND STEAMED DUMPLINGS.

I'VE BEEN COMING HERE SINCE I WAS AN EMBRYO IN MY MOTHER'S WOMB, EATING THE SAME DISHES.

COMFORT FOOD AT ITS MOST BASE.

WO HOP IS OPEN 24-HOURS A DAY IN NYC WHERE COPS AND ROBBERS CAN EAT NEXT TO EACH OTHER IN A HASSLE-FREE ZONE...

...BEFORE BREAKING THEIR EMBARGO IN THE STREETS ABOVE THIS SUBTERRANEAN HAVEN.

DON'T LET THE PERFECT GET IN THE WAY OF THE GOOD.

FOR DESSERT, THERE ARE CLASSIC VIDEO GAMES TO BE CONQUERED ACROSS THE STREET AT THE CHINATOWN FAIR VIDEO ARCADE WITH A PHOTO-BOOTH TO RECORD THE WHOLE AFFAIR.

OX OX OX

AND, WHAT KEPT THE ARCADE ARCHAIC FOR SO MANY YEARS WAS A LIVE ROOSTER THAT PLAYED TIC-TAC-TOE VIA ELECTRIC SHOCK FOR 50-CENTS A GAME.

60

However, eating in public wasn't always fun and games.

When I was a teenager, Times Square presented a mortal challenge at a Chinese food buffet——

Where a drunken Greek mobster flew off the handle for no good reason.

CRASH

Bus your tray, GAMOTO!

DIE, GAMOTO!

Scared that he was reaching for a gun to shoot my family, I dove towards the crazed man and pressed hard against his chest.

My family rallied and brought the pain with the pride and roar of a thousand mad lions.

When the proprietors called the police, it was confirmed that the Greek mobster was holding a pistol with intent to kill.

That was the day I earned my third eye and learned to expect the unexpected in the big apple.

ON MY SIXTEENTH BIRTHDAY, MY FATHER GIFTED ME A VISIT TO THE RUSSIAN-TURKISH BATHHOUSE WHERE I LEARNED TO STEEP IN HOT STEAM AND BREATHE IN THE SOOTHING OILS OF EUCALYPTUS.

I ENCOUNTERED MY FIRST FULL BODY MASSAGE WHEN A MUTE POLISH WOMAN SCRUBBED MY VERY SOUL WITH DEAD SEA-SALTS, SENDING MY MIND TO VENUS AND BACK.

I'VE BEEN BROILING IN THE HEALING FIRES OF THAT EAST VILLAGE INFERNO, EVER SINCE.

FOR 20th CENTURY NOSTALGIA, THERE'S NO BETTER PLACE TO VISIT THAN CONEY ISLAND.

HOME OF THE WONDER WHEEL, MERMAID PARADE, FREAKSHOW, POLAR BEAR CLUB, THE RECENTLY DEMOLISHED ASTROLAND (REPLACED BY LUNA PARK), AND MANY OTHER ATTRACTIONS.

INCLUDING THE CYCLONE, WHICH CONTINUES TO STAND THE TEST OF TIME AND CHALLENGES ONES CAPACITY FOR FEAR WHERE --

-- AT 55 MILES PER HOUR, YOU CAN WITNESS THE SCREWS UNHINGING AS THE ROLLER COASTER RATTLES ITS WOODEN FRAME WITH EVERY DESCENDING LOOP AND TURN.

MATCHED ONLY BY THE DEVASTATING BODY SLAMS OF THE BUMPER CAR RIDE WHERE WIT AND STEALTH IS THE KEY TO AVOIDING WHIPLASH.

IT WAS SMARTER TO SKIP THE RIDES WHERE A MAN STOOD BY WITH A BUCKET AND MOP FOR RIDER VOMIT AND, INSTEAD, PLAY SKEE BALL WHERE WINNING TICKETS SCORED YOU A CARNIVAL PRIZE.

WHEN I WAS A KID, MY FATHER WOULD VISIT THE LOCAL STEAM ROOMS WHILE THE REST OF MY FAMILY SUNBATHED AND SWAM IN THE ATLANTIC OCEAN.

MY BROTHER AND I WOULD PLAY PINBALL ON THE BOARDWALK AND EAT ICE CREAM AND FRENCH FRIES FOR LUNCH.

MY FAMILY WOULD RENDEZVOUS AT NATHAN'S HOT DOG STAND AT FIVE O'CLOCK ON THE DOT WHERE THEY STILL SERVE "CHOW MEIN ON A BUN" AND WE'D DRIVE TO WO HOP FOR DINNER.

Nathan's
WORLD FAMOUS KFURTERS SINCE 1916
TESSEN
uffet Catering

THIS IS THE
Nathan's TAKE HOME FOOD

OUR FAMILY AVOIDED DEATH, TWICE, ONE SATURDAY, WHEN MY FATHER ARRIVED FIVE MINUTES LATE, MISSING A CAR THAT CRASHED INTO NATHAN'S AND RIPPED A WOMAN'S LEG CLEAN OFF.

THEN, WE DECIDED TO LEAVE WO HOP WHEN THE LINE TO GET INSIDE PROVED TOO LONG. THAT EVENING, A GANG WAR ERUPTED ON THE PREMISES AND PEOPLE WERE MURDERED.

RISE AND SHINE.

MILK, NO SUGAR. JUST HOW YOU LIKE IT.

STEAM ROOMS, CYCLONES, AND BEEF WITH TOMATO.

MY LOVE LETTER TO NEW YORK CITY.

ALAS, THINGS HADN'T WORKED OUT FOR US. SHE STILL CARRIED A TORCH FOR AN OLD FLAME.

THANKS FOR CHECKING IN ON ME.

BE WELL.

EVEN THOUGH THE BLACKOUT WAS STILL IN EFFECT, I FELT REFRESHED.

RENEWED.

READY.

# I'D RATHER BE HAPPY THAN RIGHT

It started with the toothpaste dispenser. I noticed a dried glop of minty white fresh cement plastered against the side of the toothpaste and thought, "Linda. Not again."

Then I noticed another petty crime. The bottom portion of the toothpaste dispenser was filled with toothpaste while the middle section had been strangled of its guts. Why didn't she know to roll the toothpaste out from the bottom, pushing any excess of the dental aid towards the top of the tube so as to maximize the full employ of the contents? I actually got mad for a moment and then controlled my temper. "It's just toothpaste," I told myself. "Maybe she doesn't know that trick?"

When I went into the kitchen to pour us cups of coffee, I noticed that the sponge had moved from its home over to a different spot. Why was the sponge cater-corner to the sink and not sitting next to the dish washing liquid? "Linda" I sighed to myself. Why hadn't Linda put the sponge back where it belonged? Everything has its place. That's when I noticed the dishes and cups in the drying rack. There was a layer of grease underneath the dishes and I found a spot of dried soap on the handle of one of the cups. If I told her once, I told her a million times, you have to wash the entire dish and the entire cup and rinse them thoroughly. Not just the parts where food and drink occupy. Everyone knows that!

When I brought Linda her coffee, she smiled and gave me a kiss and said, "Thanks, honey." I didn't return her smile. Instead, I put my coffee down and said, "Linda, there's something I need to talk to you about." She sipped her coffee and I told her about the toothpaste problem and the dish debacle. She looked upset. As if she'd dropped a baby on its head, and said, "I don't think I did that." I told her it was okay and that it was no big deal but to please double check whenever she used the toothpaste or washed the dishes. I suggested that I could help her create a system that would allow her to better achieve domestic goals.

I once left the apartment and traveled three blocks before I realized that I left the coffee machine on, forgot to turn off the oven, and didn't remember to shut and lock the window by the fire escape. When I got back home, the coffee machine and oven were off. The window was locked. A false alarm. However, despite the waste of time and worry, I was happy to know that I had installed some sort of inherent system that reminded me to return things to their proper positions before heading out for the day. It gave me a sense of confidence and reduced my anxieties.

Later that day, I received a phone call from Linda, "I'm sorry. I promise to not mess up the toothpaste or the dishes again." I told her it was alright and to not think about it anymore. "These things happen."

The next night I noticed that Linda had placed the book she was reading on top of a smaller book above the bed in a way that it could possibly fall on her head in the middle of the night. It happened to me once and I was warning her of the potential disaster. She looked at me, tired and withdrawn, as I lifted and placed her bigger book underneath her smaller book in an optimal way to prevent an accident. She said "I'm sorry" and rolled over and went to sleep. I felt good about the fact that she would be able to dream sans the startling interruption of gravity challenged books.

When the police called me, I was completely unprepared. Linda had been riding her bike to work when the car hit her from behind. The bike helmet did nothing to save her head from the damage that had been done and she was gone. A lot of people came to say goodbye at her funeral and beautiful things were said. Friends and family insisted on taking me back home but I needed to be alone. I missed her so much.

A few days merged into one long deluge of uncharted limbo. I couldn't actually eat and sleep but when I managed to pass out, she was lying there, right next to me, telling me she was sorry. I felt so bad. I didn't want her to be sorry about anything. Those little things didn't mean anything in the grand scheme. Sure, forgetting to throw the tea bag in the garbage rather than let it sit and stain the ceramic mug over night wasn't the best way to preserve a cup but we could always get a new one. It wasn't about rules, it was about being practical. It was about employing shortcuts to a better quality of life. Right?

When I decided to join the land of the living, again, I walked into the bathroom and squeezed some toothpaste onto my toothbrush. I felt something old rub against my finger. It was dried toothpaste on the side of the dispenser. When the coffee machine alerted me that the coffee was brewed and ready to pour, I lifted a cup from the dry rack and it almost slipped from my grip. The ceramic handle had a little bit of grease on it. I went to grab the sponge but it wasn't where it was supposed to be. It was catercorner to the sink. I was so used to everything being in their place that I wasn't looking anymore. And then it hit me. Was it me? Was I blaming her for mistakes that I had made? Was she too nice and dignified a person to point fingers at me. Had she been taking the fall for my delinquency?

I smiled. Then I cried.

And, that's when I opened my eyes and looked around the kitchen. I saw it for the first time in months. There was the sink [which was empty], the dry rack [with the semi-clean dishes], the oven [which was off], the refrigerator [which was on], the cabinets [which were closed], the clock [which was ticking], the window [which was locked], and, then I saw the chalkboard. The chalkboard which Linda handmade and gave me a year before. The chalkboard where she would write a message to me, once in awhile, when she woke up early to go to work. Something for me to indulge and chew on for the day. So many messages were written and responded to and erased on that chalkboard. Today it said something that she had written a week ago, "Don't let the perfect get in the way of the good." ■

WHEN I LIVED IN NEW YORK'S "ALPHABET CITY" IN THE MID-1990S, THERE WAS A SCI-FI LOOKING CON ED PLANT DOWN THE BLOCK FROM ME THAT BURST FROM THE CONCRETE LIKE SOMETHING OUT OF A HORROR MOVIE.

"BZZT"

BY DEAN HASPIEL

IF YOU COULD SEE BEYOND THE HEROIN ADDLED HUMAN QUESTION MARKS HOVERING ON THEIR ONE HOOF, THE BACKDROP WAS THAT OF RED BRICK, CAGED WINDOWS, AND A ROOF LITTERED WITH METAL SPINDLES AND STEEL SPLINTERS, LIKE THE BACK OF SOME PREHISTORIC SPACE MONSTER.

THE SMELL OF BURNT RUBBER AND FRIED HAIR EMANATED FROM THE BUILDINGS EXHAUST VENTS AS THE TOXIC FUMES RADIATED MY EYES, CLOGGED MY PORES, AND BLACKENED MY LUNGS.

I HEARD THE SOUNDS OF A MACHINE SUCKING AND PUMPING CHUNKY AIR AND I WAS CONVINCED MY NEXT DOOR NEIGHBOR WAS A ROBOT SENT FROM THE FUTURE WITH A SECRET MISSION TO INSULATE THE WALLS OF LOWER EAST SIDE TENEMENTS WITH HUMAN GUTS AND BRAIN.

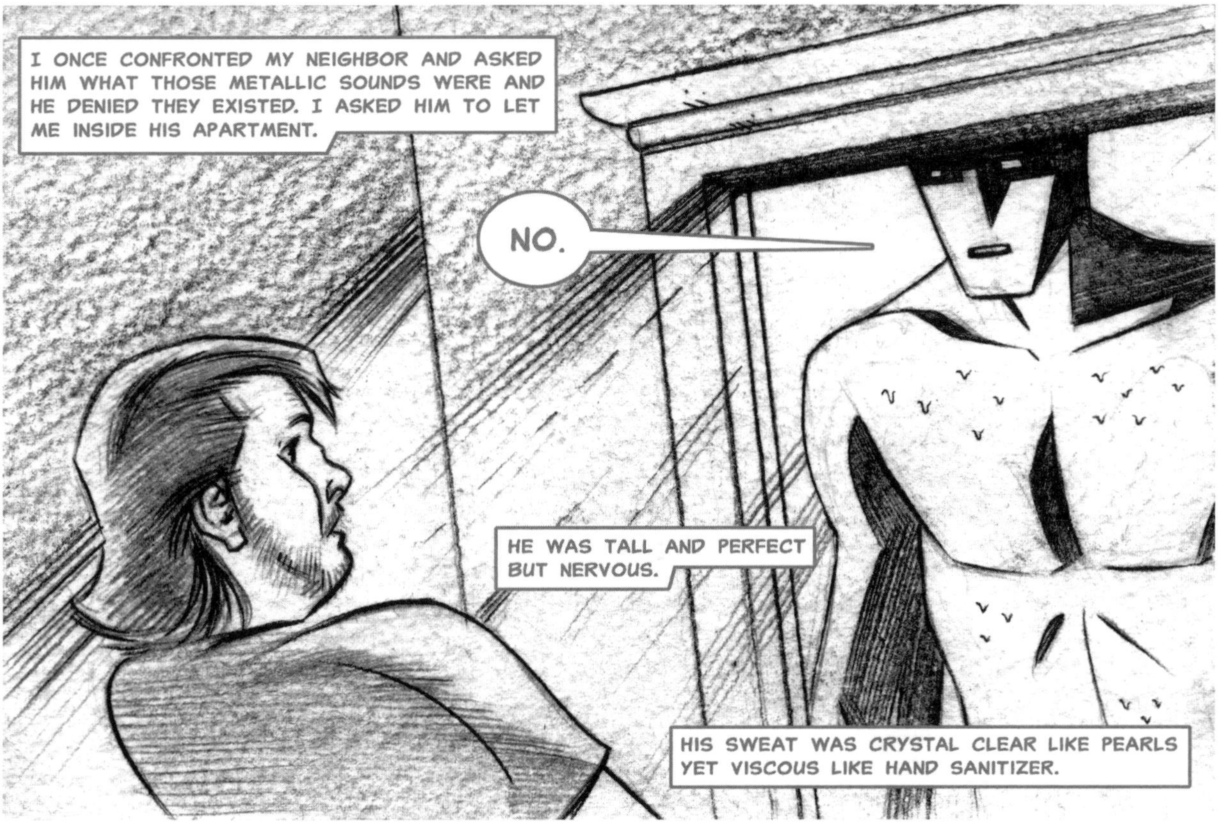
I ONCE CONFRONTED MY NEIGHBOR AND ASKED HIM WHAT THOSE METALLIC SOUNDS WERE AND HE DENIED THEY EXISTED. I ASKED HIM TO LET ME INSIDE HIS APARTMENT.
NO.
HE WAS TALL AND PERFECT BUT NERVOUS.
HIS SWEAT WAS CRYSTAL CLEAR LIKE PEARLS YET VISCOUS LIKE HAND SANITIZER.

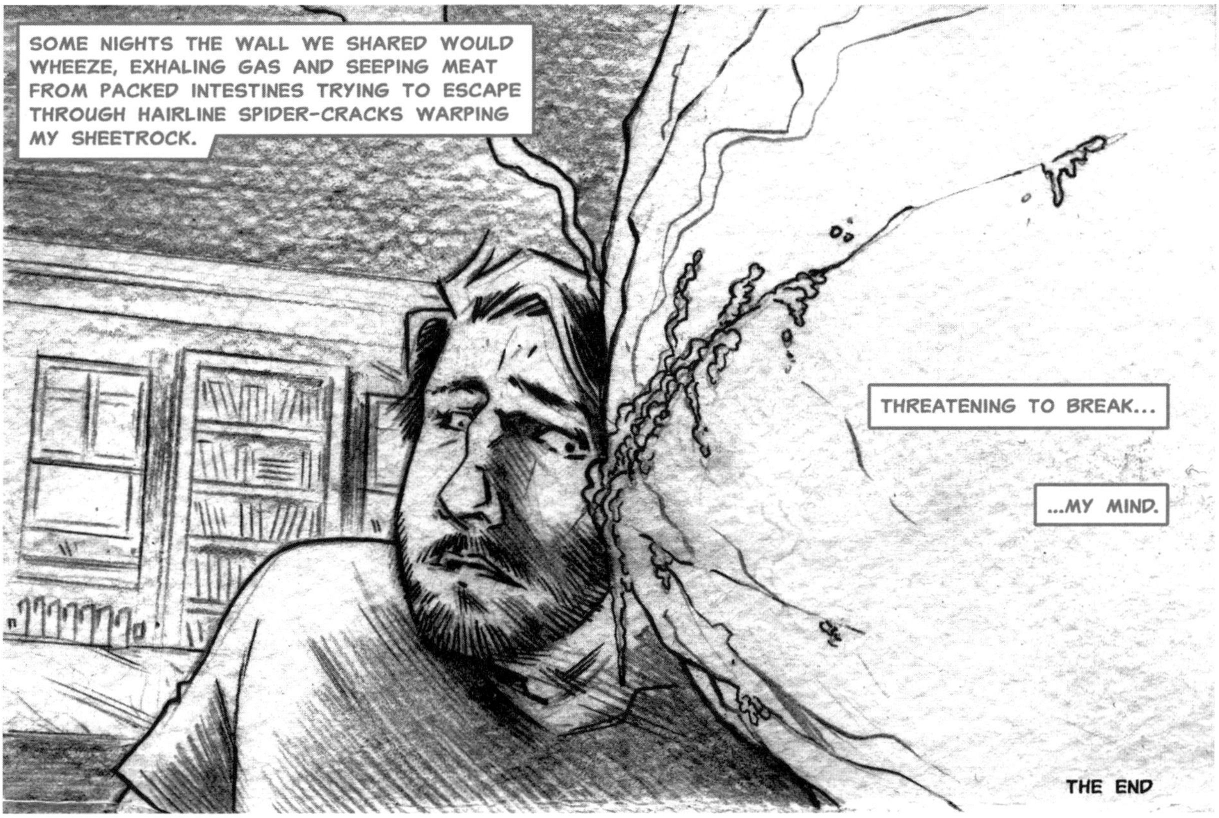
SOME NIGHTS THE WALL WE SHARED WOULD WHEEZE, EXHALING GAS AND SEEPING MEAT FROM PACKED INTESTINES TRYING TO ESCAPE THROUGH HAIRLINE SPIDER-CRACKS WARPING MY SHEETROCK.
THREATENING TO BREAK...
...MY MIND.
THE END

# THE PLATE

The only thing I had left of her were two plates. They were handcrafted with paintings of flowers glazed into the ceramic by factory kiln fire. Sentimentally obvious but oddly comforting. I even had a favorite one. I can't remember if she had them when we first started dating or if they were a gift after we moved in together. All I can remember is that she let me have them when she broke up with me after six years of dating so I would have something to eat on.

I moved across the water from her but I reconciled we were only seven subway stops and a few city blocks away from each other. She slept next to me on my futon bed the night I moved into my place to help me make the transition. It was the second to last time I ever saw her. Whenever I cooked myself a meal or ordered take-out food, I used the plate I liked better and would set the other plate next to mine. It was her plate. It was our date.

I ate like that for a year. Even when I started to date new people again. I remember the first time I served food to another woman on her plate. I felt like I was betraying her. I knew it was preposterous to feel that way but feelings have a way of dictating almost everything. But, I got used to sharing the only physical thing I had left of her and, over time, I let anyone use our plates. They were fine plates. They were strong plates. If we couldn't eat on them together anymore then I had to let them be available for others to use. They were plates.

There were other plates in the cabinet. Some were cheap. Some were made in China. Expensive plates. Disposable plates. Enough to feed twenty people. I could have had a dinner party. My then-roommate had his girlfriend over for dinner and I heard them cooking in the kitchen while I read a comic book. One of my favorite noises is the culinary sounds of people preparing food. That, and the mechanic audio of a washer and dryer cleaning and drying clothes. Especially when a rebel metal coin has dislodged from a back pants pocket and slides and catches against the sides of the circular motion of the machine, repeating that slide and catch, over-and-over, for 45-minutes straight. It's like a hypnotizing metronome that disarms and displaces me and makes me drowsy with bliss.

I was awakened to the ding of a bell in the kitchen. The timer let my room-mate and his girlfriend know that the pasta was boiled and ready for sauce as they grated Parmesan cheese and tossed a salad. The pasta was being strained of excess water when I heard the horrific smashing sound of ceramic breaking into pieces. There was a loud gasp and then bleak silence. Steam rose off the pasta and my heart sank. The sounds of a garbage can being dragged across the floor to the counter and the brushing of something substantial into the waste container was followed by a shy, "I'm Sorry." And, my fears were confirmed when I witnessed the shards of my favorite plate in the garbage.

At least her plate was safe but there was no good reason to let her phantom eat with me. The day after the death of my favorite plate, I ate alone with her plate.

Sometimes I would use other plates when I ate at home with other people. Soon enough, she disappeared when she realized that she wasn't invited to my dinner table, anymore.

When I finally fell in love with another woman, we would visit my mother in the mountains. A way to get away from the city for a weekend that sometimes felt like a vacation. We would do things country-folk sometimes do and go to yard sales and peruse other peoples things that were priced to move immediately. I remember coming across a rusty set of wide, metal plates. Each one was a different solid color. Blue, Green, Red, Yellow, Purple, Orange. Etc. They reminded me of the plates my family ate on when I was young. My mother admitted that they were our family plates and she had sold them to someone else in the mountains and now they were for sale from someone else. I couldn't believe my eyes. The entire set cost me one dollar.

I decided to eat on my family plates because they reminded me of a time when I was immortal and visiting your dreams were the reason to sleep. Before career fantasies, before real paying jobs, and before anxiety. Those family plates were from a time before I knew what a heartbreak was. Before girls. Before the truth.

When my new girlfriend broke up with me after seven years of dating, all I had left of her was a hairbrush she used and kept in my medicine cabinet in the bathroom. There were a few, pulled strands of her blonde hair caught in the plastic teeth of the brush. I contemplated mailing the hairbrush back to her or throwing it out in the garbage. I once had a dream where I rebuilt her from the DNA stored in her hairbrush. Or, was that a nightmare? It's been over three years since she left me and her hairbrush is still in the top shelf of my medicine cabinet. The hair has grown long. Does hair never die?

The other day, it was late and I was hungry. I prepared some food and opened the cabinet where all my plates were. For some reason, hers was on top. The hand-painted flower plate I was less fond of. The one that was all mine, now, because she wasn't allowed to eat with me anymore. Sure, I could've shared but I didn't. I shouldn't. I wouldn't. I couldn't. I picked up the plate and saw that there was a big, hairline crack in it. I didn't want it to break any further. So, I stopped using it and put it to the side. And, now it lays there. Waiting for food. ■

# FuNNY You SHoulD AsK!

©2005 DEAN HASPIEL

HAD I MOVED AWAY MY BODY WOULD'VE BETRAYED MY LOVE FOR HER.

SO, I LOOKED AWAY RATHER THAN AT HER FACE FOR FEAR OF LOSING MY MIND.

HER KNEE

MY STOP CAME AND AS I GOT UP TO LEAVE, SO DID SHE.

A GENTLEMAN, I LET HER GO FIRST.

I WANTED TO SEE HER BUTT.

THE STREET LAMPS MADE MY SHADOW LOOM ABOVE HERS LIKE A FRANKENSTEIN MONSTER.

SO, I SLOWED UNTIL MY SHADOW RECEDED FROM STALKER TO PEDESTRIAN.

AND THAT'S WHEN SHE STOPPED.

TURNED AROUND,

AND

SAID

DO YOU KNOW WHERE DEAN IS?

I WANTED TO TELL HER ABOUT THE WONDERFUL COINCIDENCE.

INSTEAD, I POINTED HER IN THE RIGHT DIRECTION AND LET HER OUT OF MY SIGHT.

DEAN ST

# THE LAST TIME

December is abrasive because, no matter how hard some people try to ignore the holidays, it can't be avoided. Almost everyone you know disappears and the absence of the familiar fills every corner with a specter of what you're missing. Stores close and you start to ration what you took for granted. Once bustling streets become sparse and decorations seem to personally mock you in every window. As if the city decided to throw a party and you wound up arriving before everyone else did or right after everyone left.

A week later, things start to return to normal and everyone shares their stories of what they did. You forgot to treat the holiday like a vacation and you kick yourself. That first day back to the drawing board is tough because the energy around you is infected with post-holiday withdrawal. You remain morbidly sobered by the criminal fact that you let another December hold you hostage in an emotional coma and retrace your steps to the way it was so you can inform January with the snap and verve of November. And then, Henry, your art studio landlord expresses, in very plain terms, why winter is so very different from The Fall.

"Oh, hey. How was your holiday?" Henry asks.

"Glad to be back to work. Yours?" I say.

"Good. Good. Yeah, right. Um, say, I meant to tell you..." Henry pauses, "Andy is no longer with us."

I look down at the rug between us. Where is Andy? Andy is supposed to be laying there, sleeping between us.

Henry acknowledges the empty rug, too and says, "Yeah, Andy was having a tough time getting up and down the stairs and he couldn't hold it in anymore. You saw him. You know what I'm talking about."

"I'm so sorry for your loss," I muster. "Does your son know? He was away in the Catskills...or was it the Caribbean?"

"He knows. In fact, when we decided to do it, I carried Andy over to him so they could say goodbye for the last time."

I walked back into my studio room and tried to remember the last time I saw Andy. It must have been a week ago. I would open the downstairs door. Park and lock my bicycle. Walk upstairs one flight and open the office door that led to my studio and, eight times out of ten, Andy would be sleeping on the rug and there would be a delayed reaction between the sound of the office door creaking open and his ears registering the noise. Andy's neck would crane and wake him up before his eyes would open and then he'd look to see who the intruder was. I'd say "Hi, Andy" and he would eventually acknowledge me. And slowly lower his head back into his dream. Sometimes I would pet Andy. I think he liked it when I pet his head but he had so many pink, cancerous tumors on his eyes and nose and body that I was afraid my strokes hurt him more than soothed. His back legs were shot. He could hardly walk. Andy often defecated on the rug. That's partially why the rug was there.

Other people avoided Andy like the plague but I sometimes encouraged him to get up and walk across the room so that he felt like he did something. Like it meant something. I remember witnessing Andy try to climb down a flight of steps. He practically slid and fell down the stairwell while holding onto a time when he could run down those steps with the ease of youth but now he was like an old man refusing to walk with a cane. Refusing to spend time with family and friends during the holidays. And, now he was gone.

I understood the decision to put Andy "to sleep." He slept most of the time and I wondered if waking him up when I or anybody else walked in the door, reminded him of what he couldn't do anymore and he'd rather get back to his dreams where he could walk and run and jump and play without a crutch. Now...he could fly.

I sat down at my desk and pondered the year ahead, the endless possibilities, and tried to draw something. Nothing. I tried to write. Nothing. Death does not prepare you for the reality of death. Maybe the loss of Andy got to me in a way I wasn't prepared for.

A week goes by and the streets are bustling, well, more like bumbling because it's colder and people are layered with clothes that makes them walk like large, drunken dwarfs. I'm finishing my late morning coffee and washing the dishes by my kitchen window when I notice the old lady across the street walking her dog. Something isn't right. The dog she's walking is smaller, younger. Where's her dog? The big, lanky one who looked like Marmaduke and hung out of their window and barked at me. The one dog I've waved at almost everyday the past 15-years?

And then it hit me. He was old. He was gone. Just like Andy.

Why didn't the old lady tell me? Why couldn't I have said goodbye? How do you say goodbye? It occurred to me that I didn't know the dog's name. I didn't know the old lady's name. I didn't know this family. I only waved at the dog in the window when he barked at me. That was the entirety of our 15-year relationship.

Bark. Wave. Bark. Wave. Bark. Wave. Fifteen years.

I watched the old lady bring the new puppy to the ground floor door of her building as it hesitated to enter its new home and I stared at her living room window hoping I was wrong about her old dog. I waited for him to run to the window like I saw him do whenever anyone penetrated their premises and greet them with a loud bark.

And, I waited. ∎

# MONTERO BAR & GRILL
## BY DEAN HASPIEL

WHEN I FIRST MOVED TO BROOKLYN, 15-YEARS AGO, MY PAL, ZACH, INSISTED ON TAKING ME TO THIS "REALLY COOL, REMOTE SALOON BY THE WATERFRONT" ON ATLANTIC AVENUE.

MONTERO BAR & GRILL WAS OLD, BEAUTIFUL, DECORATED WITH BLACK & WHITE PICTURES OF THE PAST, MODEL SHIPS, NAUTICAL PARAPHERNALIA, WOODEN PHONE BOOTHS (THE KIND CLARK KENT USED TO DRESS INTO SUPERMAN), A POOL TABLE, A PARROT, A JUKEBOX AND STORIES.

SO MANY STORIES.

THE FIRST TIME I WENT, MONTERO'S WAS EMPTY AND WE TALKED TO A NICE BARTENDER. BESIDES THE ANCIENT LOOK AND FEEL, I WONDERED WHY ZACH THOUGHT THIS PLACE WAS SO COOL?

THEN IT HAPPENED. A MAN STUMBLED IN FROM THE EMERGENCY ROOM ACROSS THE STREET AND SAT AT THE FIRST STOOL BY THE BAR. HIS HANDS AND HEAD WERE WRAPPED IN BANDAGES.

HE LOOKED LIKE THE UNKNOWN SOLDIER.

EXIT

THE BARTENDER EXCUSED HERSELF MID-SENTENCE, PULLED OUT A BOTTLE OF BOURBON AND A SHOT GLASS, PLACED IT IN FRONT OF THE UNKNOWN SOLDIER, AND WALKED BACK OVER TO US TO FINISH OUR CONVERSATION. ZACH GAVE ME A LOOK, "**THAT'S** WHY THIS BAR IS FRESH."

I PRACTICALLY LIVED IN MONTERO'S ON A FRIDAY NIGHT THOSE FIRST FEW YEARS IN BROOKLYN.

SO MANY STORIES.

I VOWED TO NEVER GO BACK THE NIGHT I WOKE UP THERE WITH A GLASS OF WHISKEY IN MY HAND.

MY FIRST BLACK OUT?

MANY YEARS WENT BY BEFORE I STEPPED INTO MONTERO'S AGAIN. SOME THINGS HAD CHANGED TO KEEP BUSINESS GOING, LIKE KARAOKE, BUT SOME OF THE MAINSTAYS WERE STILL THERE AND I WAS GREETED WITH A WARM WELCOME AND HUG AS IF I NEVER LEFT.

CHEERS!

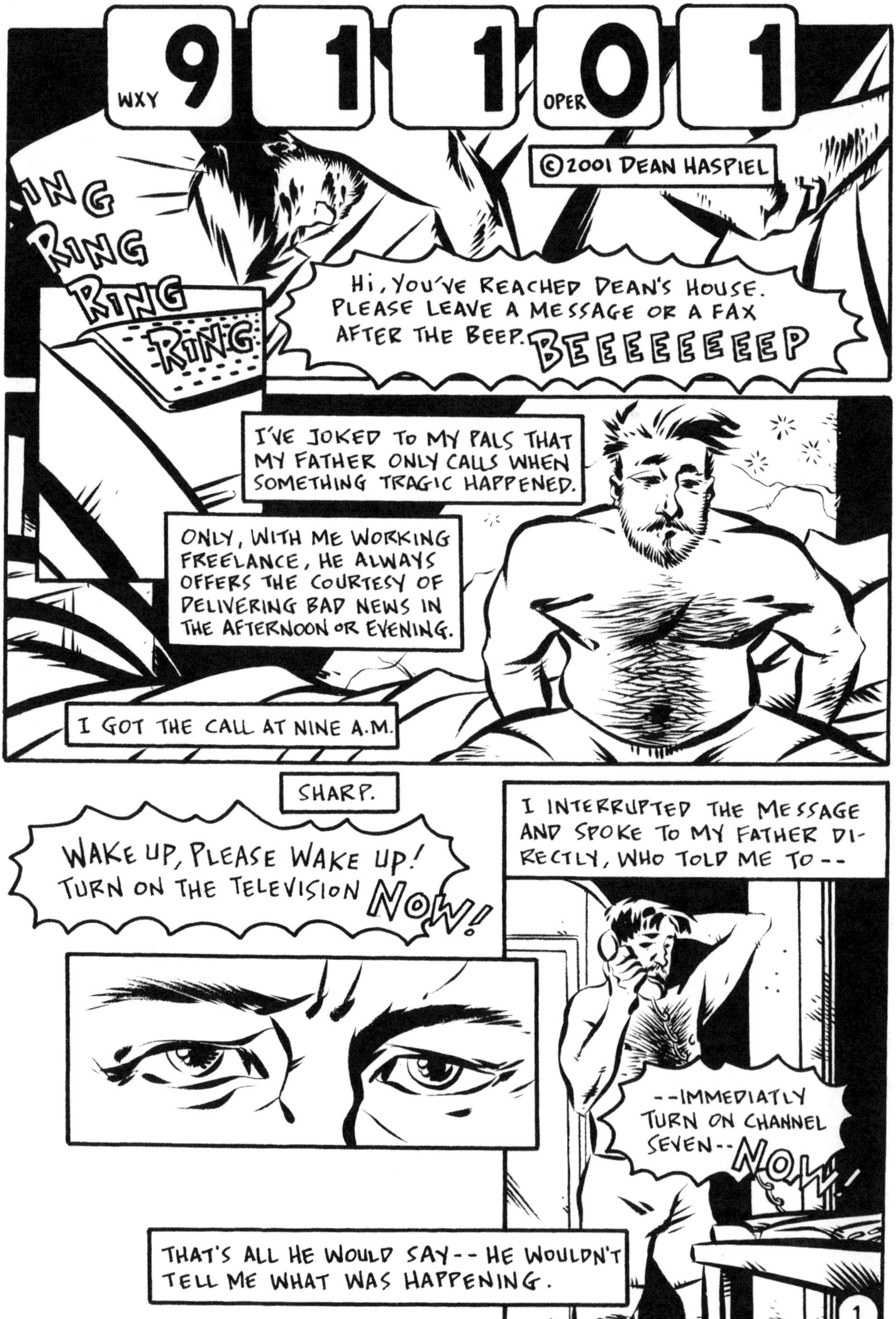
WXY 9 1 1 OPER 0 1
©2001 DEAN HASPIEL
ING RING RING RING
HI, YOU'VE REACHED DEAN'S HOUSE. PLEASE LEAVE A MESSAGE OR A FAX AFTER THE BEEP. BEEEEEEEEP
I'VE JOKED TO MY PALS THAT MY FATHER ONLY CALLS WHEN SOMETHING TRAGIC HAPPENED.
ONLY, WITH ME WORKING FREELANCE, HE ALWAYS OFFERS THE COURTESY OF DELIVERING BAD NEWS IN THE AFTERNOON OR EVENING.
I GOT THE CALL AT NINE A.M.
SHARP.
WAKE UP, PLEASE WAKE UP! TURN ON THE TELEVISION NOW!
I INTERRUPTED THE MESSAGE AND SPOKE TO MY FATHER DIRECTLY, WHO TOLD ME TO --
--IMMEDIATLY TURN ON CHANNEL SEVEN-- NOW!
THAT'S ALL HE WOULD SAY -- HE WOULDN'T TELL ME WHAT WAS HAPPENING.
1

TURNING ON THE TELEVISION, IT LOOKED LIKE A PLANE HAD HIT ONE OF THE WORLD TRADE TOWERS...

...LIKE WHAT HAD HAPPENED TO THE PAN-AM BUILDING & THE EMPIRE STATE BUILDING MANY, MANY YEARS AGO.

SO I'M THINKING "WHAT A DAMN SHAME," AND ALTHOUGH WE HAD HUNG UP THE PHONE--

--I KEPT WATCHING THE NEWS FOR A FEW MORE MINUTES, WHEN SUDDENLY--

--I WATCHED ANOTHER AIRPLANE FLY TOWARDS THE SECOND TOWER AND I'M THINKING "WAIT, WHAT'S HAPPENING?"

AND THEN--

-- BECAUSE I DON'T HAVE CABLE--

-- MY TV WENT STATIC.

NO...

2

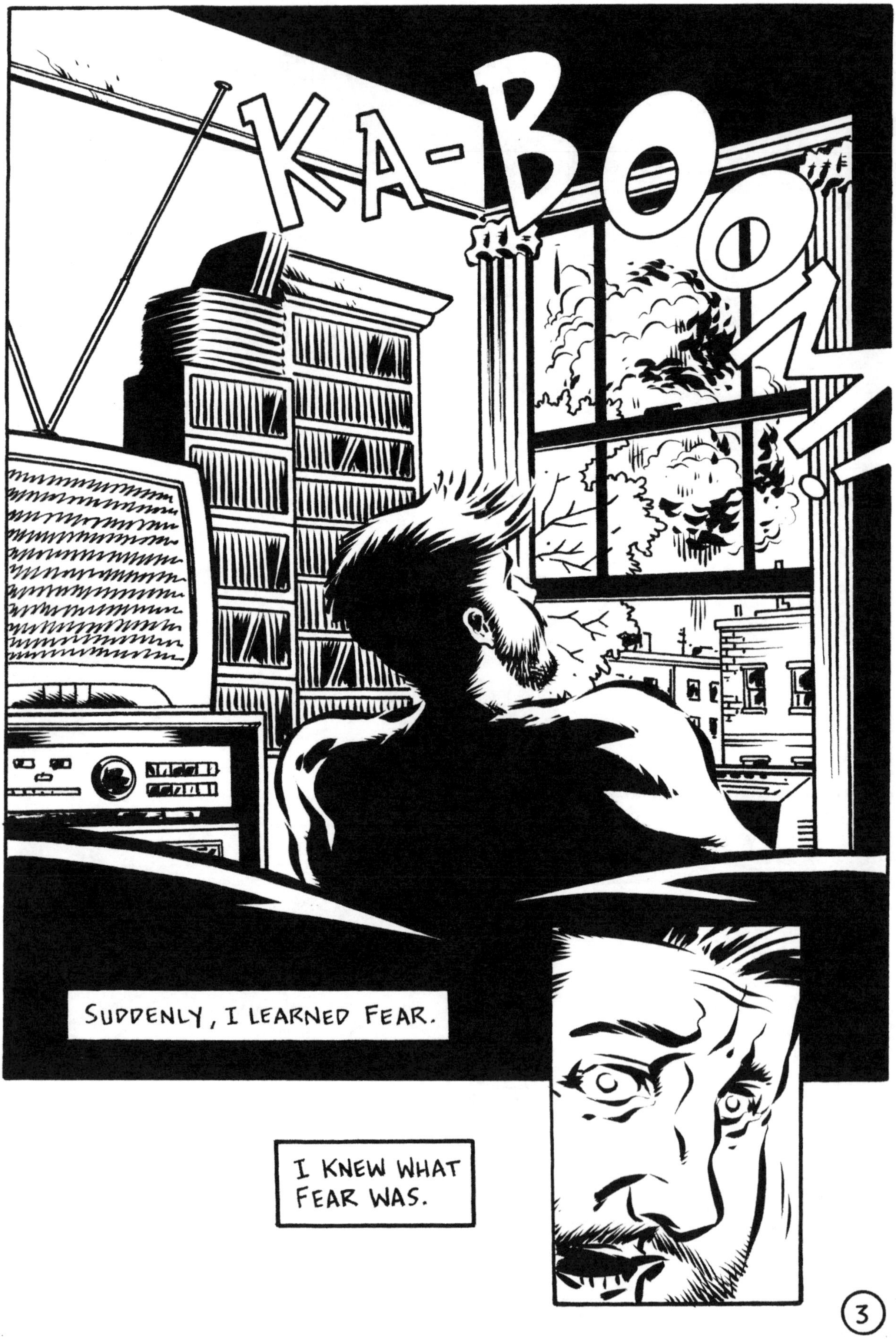
KA-BOOM!
SUDDENLY, I LEARNED FEAR.
I KNEW WHAT FEAR WAS.
3

I REALIZED SOMETHING WAS REALLY WRONG, AND SOMETHING BIGGER THAN AIRPLANES ACCIDENTALLY CRASHING INTO THE WORLD TRADE TOWERS WAS OCCURRING --

--AND THAT THIS WAS A DELIBERATE ATTACK.

I RAN TO A NEIGHBOR'S APARTMENT WHO HAD CABLE TV, AND LEARNED THAT COMMERCIAL AIRPLANES WITH INNOCENT PASSENGERS HAD BEEN HIJACKED AND TERRORISTS WERE SURGICALLY CRASHING THEM INTO IMPORTANT LANDMARKS ACROSS AMERICA.

NEXT THING WE KNEW, THERE WERE REPORTS THAT THE PENTAGON WAS HIT.

ANOTHER HIJACKED COMMERCIAL AIRPLANE WENT DOWN IN PENNSYLVANIA ...

THE APOCALYPSE...

④

BACK IN MY APARTMENT, I WAS ABLE TO TUNE IN CHANNEL 2, WHILE TALKING WITH MY PAL JOSH NEUFELD ON THE TELEPHONE ABOUT WHAT WAS HAPPENING AND WHAT HE HEARD.

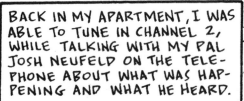

WE WATCHED IN HORROR AS ONE OF THE TWIN TOWERS STARTED TO CRUMBLE.

I...HAVE TO GO...

I COULD HEAR IT HAPPEN OUTSIDE MY WINDOW AS I WITNESSED IT FALL AND I COULD NOT BELIEVE IT.

RRRuUMMBBLe

SHORTLY THEREAFTER, THE SECOND TOWER CRUMBLED TO THE GROUND.

I WAS FREAKING OUT. I WAS HEARING REPORTS ABOUT THE CAPITOL OF OUR NATION POSSIBLY GETTING ATTACKED.

I DIDN'T KNOW WHAT WAS HAPPENING ANYMORE.

I FELT SOMETHING I HAD NEVER FELT BEFORE--

--WAR IN AMERICA.

5

CARROLL GARDENS WAS IN THE DIRECT PATH OF THE WIND AND IT STARTED TO SNOW ASH.

I COULD SMELL SMOKE AND BURNT PLASTIC AND OTHER ...THINGS...

SOOT COVERED THE CARS AND THE BUILDINGS AND THE STREETS BELOW, EVERYTHING IN LAYERS, AS PEOPLE RAN, COVERING THEIR EYES & MOUTHS FROM THE HUMAN DETRITUS & DEBRIS.

BURNT DOCUMENTS CAME FLOATING IN THROUGH MY KITCHEN WINDOW --

-- FROM AN OFFICE IN THE WORLD TRADE CENTER ACROSS THE RIVER.

THE PHONE RANG.

AND RANG.

AND I WAS AFRAID.

6

# THE ICEBOX

My girlfriend had broken up with me and it tore me apart. Four weeks of post-separation anxiety slogs by and I'm struggling through another sad silent night at home alone when she calls me. I can see her name light up in my cell phone caller ID. It's really her! I'm so happy and excited, thinking she misses me and wants to reconcile. I answer and deliver a month old, "Hello." Picking up where we left off. She doesn't answer me back. Instead, I hear laughter and what sounds like her walking outside with another man. There's indecipherable pillow talk, high heeled footsteps, and more laughter. I realize that she butt-dialed me and now I'm privy to her date.

Rather than close my cell phone and walk away from the horror of her woo, I elect to listen and get upset. She sounds like she's having the time of her life as I reach into my refrigerator icebox and pull out the remnants of mint chocolate chip ice cream and slowly deplete the paper pint of its contents until, after 45-minutes, her phone miraculously turns off [runs out of battery?] and spares me from jumping out of my 3rd story window. Ice cream gone, girlfriend gone, I curl up into a ball and die.

In my death throes, I'm reminded of a different break up from a different time and how my upstairs neighbor, Seth, who I also went to high school and college with, helped get me through that rough time. When I was very single, Seth and I would rendezvous a few times a week; get take-out food and rent a video and watch it at his place. The chatter, Chinese food and cinema, helped me to heal and move on. Seth had a good shoulder to cry on.

The next day, I wake up emotionally scathed but alive and decide to see if Seth wants to reignite our old routine. I knock on Seth's door and it takes him longer than it usually does to greet me. He opens his door and has a look on his face like he's distracted and says, "Hey. What's up?"

"Food and a movie?" I encourage. Seth looks at me and squints. He's seen that face before. Heartbreak. "My treat," I offered. "Sure. Yeah, that would be cool," Seth says.

We kill five minutes discussing what kind of food we want to eat. I lean towards Chinese but Seth wants Italian and I try to convince him to split the difference and opt for Thai or Mexican. Seth suggests a good burrito place nearby but then I have a sudden hankering for Chicken Tikka Massala and we debate the pros and cons of eating beans versus curry and what that would do to our bowels halfway through whatever movie we pick to rent and watch. And then we start talking about what movies we want to see and what genre and so on and so forth. Finally I say, "Let's quit dilly-dallying and go get food and a flick before all the stores shutter for the night."

Seth grabs his coat and house keys and starts to shut the door when he realizes that he forgot something and tells me to "Hold on a minute." I watch Seth walk over to his refrigerator, open the icebox door, and pull out his phone. I can hear tiny sounds of ranting and raving, like shrieking banshees from another dimension. Seth lifts the phone to his mouth and says, "Uh-huh...uh-huh." And repeats those conciliatory grunts a few times before placing the phone next to the frozen pizza and ice water trays and slams the icebox door. He walks back over to me.

"What the hell was that?" I ask. Seth reveals, "My girlfriend and I have been arguing the last half-hour and I can't get one damned word in."

"That's cold." I say. "She's just yelling at you the whole time?"

Seth shrugs, locks his front door, and says, "What if I pick the food and you pick the drama?" ■

# CANNIBAL SATIVA

## BY DEAN HASPIEL

I WAS BLOTTO ON MALT LIQUOR WHEN I SMOKED MY VERY FIRST HIT OF MARIJUANA.

WHILE "HIGH," I WATCHED DAVID LYNCH'S *ERASERHEAD* WHEN THE SCENE WITH THE CREEPY RADIATOR LADY AND HER BULGING CHEEKS CAME ON, DOING HER SLOW TAP DANCE WHILE DODGING FALLING ABORTIONS OR WHATEVER THE HELL THOSE DEMONIC DROPPINGS WERE!

I WENT BANANAS AND NEARLY JUMPED SEVEN STORIES OUT OF MY UPPER WEST SIDE APARTMENT WINDOW.

IT WASN'T UNTIL MY FRESHMEN YEAR OF COLLEGE THAT I GOT STONED AGAIN.

THIS TIME, I SPARKED A GNARLY RUMOR THAT I'D SACRIFICED A GOAT FROM A NEARBY FARM AND STUFFED ITS HEAD IN MY REFRIGERATOR.

I COERCED SEVERAL STUDENTS TO VIEW MY "SACRIFICE" AND LET ONE CHUMP IN AT A TIME LIKE AT THOSE CIRCUS FREAK ACTS.

MOST OF THE LIGHTS IN MY ROOM WERE CUT OFF AND I'D BEND DOWN IN THE DARK, HOLD MY NOSE, OPEN THE FRIDGE DOOR, WAVE FAKE STENCH WITH MY FREE HAND, GAG FROM THE PHANTOM ROTTEN MEAT, LET THEM THINK THEY SAW THE GOAT HEAD FOR A SPLIT SECOND, AND SLAM THE FRIDGE DOOR SHUT.

MY THESPIAN SKILLS WERE OSCAR AWARD WORTHY BECAUSE THEY WOULD GET NAUSEOUS AND RUN AWAY, SPREADING CAMPUS RUMORS ABOUT MY IMPROMPTU DORM ROOM CULT.

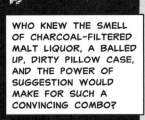

WHO KNEW THE SMELL OF CHARCOAL-FILTERED MALT LIQUOR, A BALLED UP, DIRTY PILLOW CASE, AND THE POWER OF SUGGESTION WOULD MAKE FOR SUCH A CONVINCING COMBO?

A WEEK LATER, THE DEAN OF DISCIPLINE ASKED TO TALK WITH ME AND I HAD SOME EXPLAINING TO DO.

WHEN I GOT LOOSELY ACCLIMATED TO MARIJUANA, I REALIZED IT JUST PUT ME TO SLEEP AND I WAS MORE INTERESTED IN CLIMBING THE WALLS.

I GAVE UP THE GANJA.

THE END

# SCATOLOGICAL

It started when I heard suspicious noises coming from behind my university bedroom door. It was late and I was trying to get some sleep for the next days round of film classes. Something was awry and I wondered which one of my roommates in J51, a house with a roll call made up of filmmakers, cartoonists, and musicians, friends I'd known since high school, was being shady? I hopped out of bed and swung open the door only to confront my two pals, Raf & Cooly, hunched over a section of tabloid spread across the length of my door jamb.

"The hell, man?"

Cooly looked spooked as Raf keeled over in a fit of giggles. Quick interrogation revealed a dare that Cooly would crap on a newspaper and leave it in front of my door the entire night in hopes of fumigating my olfactory with his foul feces, better yet, perhaps to get me to step in said matter come morning.

"The hell, man?"

Busted. The plan was derailed and the three of us entered the kitchen for some malt liquor to chase back the night when Dave, our resident beefcake amateur pugilist cum Herman Melville connoisseur, swung open the front door and joined us for a toast. We cheered to everything and anything whenever Olde English 800 appeared and this was no damn different. Dave had an infectious laugh and so when I told him what Raf & Cooly tried to do to me, his laughter had all of us rolling and grabbing gut. This woke people up.

The first sleep challenged casualty to climb down from upstairs in his robe was Clak, a man who carried a thousand year library in the back of his head, who didn't care why we were laughing nor did he want to share in any toast. Clak wanted milk. The next body to appear was Blazm, a witty fireplug of a man who also found the devious attempt to attack my senses quite funny. He raised a glass. Finally, Blue, the high-tech mercenary of the group wondered what the sudden gathering was all about as he pulled on a hit of Ol' E. The dare was discussed as we analyzed who could pull such a stunt if push came to shove and machismo got aggro. This was symptomatic of J51 and usually snowballed into something crazy. Often the instigator of such bad behavior, tonight I would become the victim.

I don't know if Raf winked at Cooly or if Cooly slipped a mickey in Dave's drink but within seconds Clak, Blazm, and I, were trapped inside the small kitchen area being held hostage by the trio of pranksters. Blue was on the outside of the kitchen exit playing politics. Somehow, a gauntlet was thrown down and Dave picked it up and was going to crap on the floor. The only thing that would free us was if we three caught said Dave doodoo as it poured from his anus before it hit kitchen tile.

"The hell, man?"

None of us were going to have this as we abruptly made for the exit only to have a wall of Dave, Raf & Cooly, beat us back. Dave was a Juggernaut of muscle and Cooly was a short Hulk wrapped in Wolverine rage. Raf's wiry conviction held us at bay like Plastic Man. We fought and we scrapped to no yield. By this time, Blue had run upstairs and come back down with a video camera, recording the domestic terrorism. He was laughing, too, the punk.

Dave pulled down his shorts, hovered over our extended circle of hands, and tried to poop. The sounds of him straining was appalling. None us planned to catch his crap but we egged him on, anyway. More pushing. Nothing. Dave tried again and feared urinating. All the forced pushing on his bladder was going to make him pee. He didn't want to pee. Finally, another internal shove of the intestine revealed something of a turtlehead. He yelled, "It's poking." We quickly retrieved our circle of palms in fear of catching said turtlehead when Dave pulled up his shorts, stood back up, and quit the contest. He simply couldn't shit for fear of spraying the floor with his urine.

Cooly got cocky and pulled his pants down. By hook or by crook we were going to catch crap before the night was over! Extra pumped and red in the face, Dave was upset he couldn't perform and stood tight lipped and akimbo, blocking the exit. Raf entered a new phase of conviction as he, too, blocked the exit like a human spider-web. Blue snickered as he stood on the sidelines like a war journalist, video taping the entire event, hopping up and down like a jackal. Once again, we were instructed to extend our palms below Cooly's balls and anus. Once again, we did as we were told. It didn't take long for Cooly's sphincter to pucker and slowly unload brown yogurt. Naturally, Blazm, Clak, and I, quickly withdrew our hands as shit splattered against the floor.

Then, Cooly snapped.

Bug-eyed and frothing at the mouth, Cooly grabbed a fist full of his poop and screamed, "Show me your hands!" Blazm was closest and he lied, convincing Cooly he caught it by showing the palms of his lily white clean hands. Somehow, this ploy worked as cross-eyed Cooly let Blazm go and turned his attention towards Clak and I. Clak hid behind my body as I desperately tried to pry open a boarded up section of the kitchen counter that entered another room for escape but to no avail. Cooly barked "Did you catch my crap!?" With tears in my eyes I admitted, "No!"

Shit storm soufflé.

Brown beads of wet bits and pieces got caught in my chest hairs like black Velcro and I gagged. My throat filled with saliva, preparing for a flume of vomit, and I became instantly dizzy. Clak screamed behind me as Cooly blasted another load and I staggered out of the kitchen and over to the bathroom and into the shower. I put on the hot water as bile ejected from my throat and slid down my face. Now I knew why there was water in the toilet. It helps cut the smell so you don't hurl on your lap while taking a dump.

Minutes later, I dried off and staggered back into the foyer between the bathroom and kitchen and I see the main door to the housing unit is wide open. It's like a bomb went off inside and everyone spilled outside. Dazed and stunned, everybody collects at ground zero.

A very late Larry, our resident genius writer and missing final piece to the J51 puzzle, came prancing through the front door. He smelled something rank and wondered what happened? We filled him in as we forgave the perpetrators. If there's one thing I learned from living at J51, sometimes a good story has to be lived in order to tell it. No permission. No apologies.

Larry starts laughing, certainly glad he wasn't involved when Clak decides its time to hit the hay. As he turns to leave Larry's eyes widen in disgust as he points at the back of Clak's neck, nearly puking at the evidence. Closer inspection reveals a nugget of Cooly's dung clinging to the short hairs on Clak's neck like a happy little leach. Screaming, Clak runs upstairs to lance the offensive dingleberry and everybody starts cracking up, except for me. I hurry back to the bathroom gagging and spitting up. Again.

Finally, Blue kicks himself because he pressed the pause button when he meant to press the record button on his video camera. Nothing of this harrowing event was captured. The entire night becomes hearsay. ■

# "WHAT YOU SEE IS WHAT YOU GET"
## BY DEAN HASPIEL

WHEN ME AND SOME OTHER ARTISTS DECIDED TO FORM A STUDIO IN GOWANUS, I INSTANTLY FELL IN LOVE WITH THE VIEW OF STEEL GIRDERS UNDERNEATH THE ELEVATED SUBWAY.

IT REMINDED ME OF THE ART OF ONE OF MY FAVORITE CARTOONISTS, WILL EISNER, WHO CREATED *THE SPIRIT* AND LOVED TO DRAW THE CITY.

THE LOVE AFFAIR STARTED TO DWINDLE WHEN I HEARD THE SOUND OF A VAN SCREECH TO A HALT, RIP OPEN ITS RUSTY DOOR, THROW OUT A BLOODY MATTRESS AND SPEED OFF.

THIS HAPPENED SEVERAL TIMES.

MY ROMANCE WITH THE VIEW TOOK ITS TOLL WHEN I HEARD A WOMAN SCREAM "MURDER!" AND KENNY, A HARMLESS ALCOHOLIC WHO HUDDLED AROUND THE CORNER IN A DERELICT TRUCK WITH HIS DOG, WAS STABBED SEVERAL TIMES IN THE CHEST AND FACE WHILE FIGHTING FOR HIS STOLEN SHOPPING CART.

I CALLED THE POLICE AND THEY CAUGHT THE PERPETRATORS. KENNY WENT TO THE HOSPITAL FOR SEVERAL MONTHS AND THE NEIGHBORHOOD TOOK CARE OF HIS DOG.

WHEN HE CAME BACK HOME, KENNY WAS HAPPY AND SOBER.

A FEW WEEKS LATER HE DIED OF A HEART ATTACK.

WHEN I GOT THE CHANCE TO DRAW IN A SMALL ROOM OVER A PROMINENT BOOK STORE IN THRIVING BOERUM HILL, I TOOK IT.

AT NIGHT, I COULD HEAR AUTHORS PERFORM THEIR BOOKS AND READERS SLURPING WINE AND TRADING GOSSIP.

EVENTUALLY, I WOUND UP BACK AT THAT GOWANUS ART STUDIO AND TOOK A ROOM WITH A VIEW AWAY FROM STRANGERS.

DiNO!
2013

# THE ARTISTS' COLONY

I had forgotten how much I enjoyed sitting at the head of a long dinner table at the mansion until I was granted a second residency at the legendary artists colony in upstate New York. It wasn't because I demanded an audience or that the seat positioned me in a way to judge my subjects; fellow writers, artists, filmmakers and composers, like a Game of Thrones. No, I simply enjoyed my perch to survey the lay of the land and expose myself to as many different conversations as possible. I craved the psychedelic fruits a dinner table like this one would bear. Despite the works that recommended us, we were a timid yet curious bunch with a communal commitment to communicate with strangers. With the rotating nature of residencies and artists coming and going, the chances of bonding with people are rare but it happens. Every concentration of artists yields a particular brand of eccentricity and every eccentric has its encounters...

There was the buzz-headed poet from a coal mining town with a thousand yard sneer whose first grizzled words to me were "I know who...YOU...are," while sipping from the curled straw of a carnival cup filled with vodka. Transfixed to uncover what prompted his ire, we discussed the work of mine he was familiar with and danced around the pain of a mutual pal he was at odds with. I have to admit I was energized to have been cornered by this confrontation my first night. Where most folks traded inaugural pleasantries and basked in the serene vista from the patio, I was thrown head first into the lions den. Buzz had dispensed polite jests for blunt jousts to get to the meat of matters or, more precisely, to suck out the bone marrow and spit it out. A few days later, Buzz gave a reading and his poetry was so bleak it was beautiful. The way he composed a sentence stung my soul. I found myself coping with the apocalypse of his family disasters and heartbreaks by crying while concurrently laughing like when my father took me to see a revival of William Friedkin's "The Exorcist" when I was ten years old. Shortly thereafter, Buzz gave me an excerpt from the memoir he was writing and, upon reading it, I was artistically castrated. I nearly packed my bags and hailed a bus to I'm Not Worthyville. Like fire, the wheel, and refrigeration, Buzz was a revelation. A word warrior dispatched from the annals of the suicidal heart to warn us of the cost of love and life.

Then, there was the shirtless poet with the Greg Brady hair who wondered why I sometimes spoke about myself in second-person as "Deenie-Weenie." I told him it was important to bring levity to most any social situation and what better way to break ice and set the tone than to make fun of myself. Plus, there was something about the swagger of my faux-bravado that made some people uncomfortable and I figured I would diffuse it by promoting a self-emasculating nickname. I proposed that vulnerability was the key to unlocking an honest discourse. When Greg Brady refused to play ping pong with me a second time because I "wasn't good enough" for him, I felt insulted. Suddenly, honesty wasn't my friend. The next time I sat at the dinner table he asked me why I didn't call myself "Papa Weenie." I asked "Why Papa? Is it because I'm sitting at the head of the table like a patriarch?" He corrected me and said, "Pop. A. Weenie. Get it?"

My writer's room was set inside an enclosed pine porch in front of a butter pecan colored house with chocolate trim that I also slept in. My 180 degree view was mostly littered with trees that were spotted with hidden pockets of a dilapidated tennis court, the arts colony office, a blue house west of mine, and the swimming pool that a famous author kindly gifted to his future fellows. The same swimming pool I dove naked into my first night to shed shyness and make a splash. The same swimming pool I encountered an Asian poet who rubbed her leg against mine under the water and yelped, "Ew, I touched you. You're disgusting!" I felt humiliated and publicly vowed, "I'm not going to talk to you for the entire time I'm here!" Like my scourge was supposed to banish her into the woods among the deer and ticks. It didn't occur to me until I told a friend what happened that she might have been flirting and realized a retreat also allowed adults to regress back to elementary school when we fought basic attraction and acted like brats. There were a few residents who were polyamorous or in "open marriages" or experiencing the crisis of a romantic cross-road but I didn't sense that coming from her. I gave her a second chance to be chums when she divulged personal stuff over lunch that humanized her and all animosity was lost. Artists are super-sensitive spirits who sometimes have a tough time with social formalities. Something I'm quite familiar with. I've joked that I have a special kind of social Tourette syndrome but I recognize that we are trying to make meaningful connections with our work despite public flustering. There being an ample platoon of poets spilling their guts at this particular residency, we turned our talk to poetry, which I know so little of. After I got a better sense of the medium, I suggested she curate a collection and call it "Embarrassing Humping Motions." She laughed and declared all poetry was embarrassing humping motions.

A week later, the Asian poet gave a reading in the music room which was lined with pews and stained glass windows and looked like a church. I joked with her that I could warm up the crowd with a piano tune and she took me up on it. I don't know how to perform anything musical but they chuckled when I mangled "Mary had a little lamb" three different ways. I challenged the composers in the music room to play their own versions. After the poet read variations of a Brother's Grimm tale in sonnet form, one of the composers admitted that he'd been stirred by my challenge and I encouraged him to play. He tickled out a few brilliant versions of "Mary had a little lamb" and I pushed him to transition that tune into the Charlie Brown theme which he performed imperiously. After he played more flawless mash-ups of 'Mary had a Charlie Brown,' I prompted him to shift the mash-up into a third tune and he flexed his piano fingers with a rendition of something German and classical and fierce. We were mutually elated by the manna of improvisation.

There was a woman with black fringe bangs and cat-eyeglasses who looked like a Gothic version of Velma from Scooby Doo, who tried to woo small groups of people into live action role playing games with renditions of "Arm Sex," where two consensual adults could sensually yet safely turn each other on. "It wasn't really cheating," she said. I tried to spark an arm sex threesome and recruited a charming writer from Chicago who looked like Hollywood actor Billy Zane's test-tube baby, but he was more into the experiment than she was. Maybe it was too awkward or too humid? We were experiencing a hell of a summer heatwave accentuated by the might of a million mosquitoes, after all. Gothic Velma was a conflict of provocation and boundaries who promoted a quality control manifesto of come hither and halt. It was more frustrating than freeing. A week later, she read an excerpt from the memoir she was writing about her family history with a deadly hereditary disease and how she never thought about the future because she was told there probably wouldn't be one, and I was crushed. Suddenly, her desire to LARP (Live Action Role Play) made sense. In my mind, she was trying to concurrently live multiple lives in the short time allegedly given to her, adding a hundred years to her compromised thirty. I'm not a religious man but I can easily slip into spirituality (thanks to the cosmic comic books of Jack Kirby) and, that night, I said a prayer for Gothic Velma that a tsunami of disease-free tomorrows would come flooding her way.

Whenever I was in a creative slump, I studied the squirrels, chipmunks, frogs, birds, hawk, geese, and groundhogs, who, as my girlfriend once identified, "look like they wear baggy pajamas," as they scrambled and hunted for food on the green lawn mere inches from my writers window. I often saved my required lunch pail rations of cut carrots for the animals in hopes of making friends. And, when wild life failed to inspire me, I would ride a bike around the dirt trails and over to the back end of a horse race track and by the fish pond or walk over to the blue house and listen to the staccato of an old typewriter machine. There was an older author who had been coming here for 37-years and written episodes of a cult vampire soap opera in the 1960s, and now he was writing a libretto with one of the residencies composers. The ambiance of his typewriting was like an inspiring symphony of vowels tapping away at the air that made me imagine a time when the colony was a theater of competing typewriters. Fiction versus Non-fiction. Novels versus poetry. Truth versus lies, and so on. Before wireless laptop computers gave way to the internet and spawned the time suck of social networking; where Googling your name became the birth control of creation.

One of my housemates was a Jamaican woman with gray dreadlocks who had been raised in England but eventually rejected its classism to return back to her roots in Jamaica, only to discover that she had none. We discussed the idea of home and she realized she never had one. I said to her, "Don't they say home is where the heart is?" She politely nodded but had trouble reconciling the fact that she would be returning to a small plot of land with no electricity, no contact with the outside world, to write the rest of her second novel in long-hand form because she was no longer interested in a digitized earth. I could tell being at an artists colony was a great departure for her, as it was for me, but where I would return to my first world problems in Brooklyn, NY and catch up on a month of unpaid bills and unread comic books, she would be going back to a tent in Jamaica to dig in and grow her roots, one potato at a time.

Besides the author/poetry readings in the mansion, there were several evenings of open studios where visual artists showed their work and composers played their music. They almost always transitioned into dance parties and late night pool house shenanigans. But, rather than host a solo reading of my own, I decided to curate two impromptu salons in my living room space by assembling willing talent into sharing the stuff they were currently working on and/or read published work. There was the Nigerian with an infectious laugh who read a sad poem about the night his wife left him. There was a bearded Brazilian who could keep any object in the air for long stretches of time with the power of his feet and he read a poem about flowers and sex. There was Junior Bacchus, a Midwest poet whose right hand was a bottomless cocktail and he read ditties about flying chevrons and drinking with demigods. The pigtailed Australian cum Texan who sometimes wrote at the local coffee shop or steeped in lawn chair inspiration by the poolside, read poems about puberty and pop culture and how a particular horror movie recontextualized itself over the years. The blonde from Ohio read slaughterhouse poetry about her pedophile father and the drunks she slung drinks to. The sassy writer from Arkansas read a touching story about the rise and demise of an ex-lover and, later on, belted out a rebel yell that ricocheted around the 400-acre colony with her siren. Gothic Velma read more excerpts from her memoir including, in acute detail, the chilling medical procedure of an early 1800s mastectomy that made people dizzy. Billy Zane's charming test tube baby brought the room to a roar when he read an omnipotent story about loyalty. And, Buzz read select chapters from his memoir that gobsmacked the room. I read a few short stories about loss and the first scene from my screenplay. And, I convinced a kind composer, a maestro who generously gave me recordings of his haunting music, to reveal a funny artists colony myth to prove that just about anyone could spin a good yarn.

I don't remember why but someone mentioned Wisconsin at the salon and it reminded me of a story my father told about our family that I never wrote down. So, I shared it. I was young and my native New York City family was invited by Wisconsin friends to their farm for a getaway weekend. It was the first time I ever saw the big blue sky from one end of my peripheral vision to the other. It was vast, all encompassing, and majestic. Born and bred in a city of skyscrapers, I'd never seen that much unexpurgated sky before. The Wisconsin family had a bespectacled son who was born with Osteogenesis Imperfecta, a rare bone disease that basically makes it impossible for ten year old boys to throw baseballs or play hide-and-go-seek without snapping a femur or a rib or worse. Me and my brother literally walked on egg shells while trying to navigate fun with the brittle boy. The entire weekend the brittle boy kept teasing us about an amazing thing that had just arrived in town, as if it were the eighth wonder of the world, and he couldn't wait to show us. He really sold the mystery well and I was beside myself with anticipation. Finally, the day arrives to reveal the amazing thing and our two families converge in town at a two-story tall department store. We enter the main hall and the brittle boy, so excited I was worried that he was going to break in half, points at the thing he's been wanting to show us for days. I look. I can't see it. I look towards my brother. He can't see it, either. I look at my mother for counsel and she's having trouble identifying it, too. I wanted to ask the brittle boy what I was supposed to be looking at; but, instead I looked at my father in hopes of anchoring me, and he too was rudderless until—like a beacon of light—he saw what it was that was supposed to blow our minds and immediately pretended to be in shock and awe. I follow the train of discovery between my father's eyes and the mysterious object and landed my own eyes upon...an escalator. A stairway machine that transports people between two floors (in case you didn't know). I'd seen a hundred escalators back home in Manhattan. Where was the eighth wonder of the world? I stood mute and disappointed until my father began to "ooh and ahh" as he walked towards the escalator and rode it up and down with the brittle boy, relating to his joy. I learned an important lesson that day: one person's escalator was another person's blue sky.

My residency goal was to finish a few comic book deadlines, germinate new ideas, and revisit the feature length screenplay and novel I started writing the last time I was gifted the privilege to hide away from the world. A privilege to be among a small group of select artists blessed with a brief amount of time to develop their passions, scrutinize their work and themselves while being fed, sheltered and encouraged to create sans judgment by arts conscious patrons, dedicated organizers, and a generous staff. I thought more about home and what the Jamaican woman said about roots. And, that's when I remembered a rap lyric by Eric B & Rakim, "It's not where you're from it's where you're at." I was upstate at the prestigious artists colony but I'm from New York City. Who I am is what I make. I am my comic books, my essays, my unproduced screenplays, and my unfinished novel. I help rally small tribes of artists to sit together and share something unique whether it's at a retreat in the mountains, online, or in a shared art studio in Brooklyn. I am the bashful jerk who jumps naked into the deep end of a pool to make new friends while making fun of myself so we can make fun of ourselves yet not be afraid to artistically express something meaningful and honest. And, that is my home. Wherever I am. ■